storykeepers

storykeepers

edited by Marion Halligan

DUFFY & SNELLGROVE
SYDNEY

Centenary of Federation

This project has been
supported by the
National Council for the
Centenary of Federation

Published by Duffy & Snellgrove in 2001
PO Box 177 Potts Point NSW 1335 Australia
info@duffyandsnellgrove.com.au

Distributed by Pan Macmillan

© Text: the authors 2001
© Images: see full list p 280

Cover design by Alex Snellgrove
Cover image photographed by George Serras,
© National Museum of Australia 2001
Typeset by Cooper Graphics
Printed by Hyde Park Press

A Centenary of Federation project in association with the
Word Festival of Canberra and the National Museum of Australia

ISBN 1 876631 10 4

www.duffyandsnellgrove.com.au

contents

introduction

Once upon a time … the phrase is a code that brings a multitude of small exhortations and large promises with it. They are of a kind that may seem ambivalent and even paradoxical. As of course they are. The point about stories is the immense scope for ambiguity they offer, with no need to explain it away. It's there to be enjoyed, and we as human beings have been very good for a very long time at enjoying highly complex stories.

The small exhortations: sit down, or sit up. Pay attention. Relax. Listen. Call up your imagination. Suspend your disbelief. You are being invited to an intimate act.

And the promise is, I am going to tell you a story.

There are elements of magic in this, and it's not just the association with fairy tales. It's partly to do with the odd syntax. *Once upon a time* … what time? When? And the answer is, a particular time, but also all time. Then, but still now. It belongs to our childhood, when stories always began like that, but it has not lost its power over adults.

Once upon a time … there was a little girl called Marion who lived in a house by the sea with her mummy and her daddy. One day her daddy told her a story. He said that her mummy was growing a baby in her tummy and that one day she would have a little baby brother or perhaps a little sister …

Did my father announce my sister's arrival like this? I don't remember. But he did turn my life into a narrative from time to time. The best stories are those in which we are the heroes. In nations as well as families. Purveyors of those computer-generated children's books which insert your child's name in the text know this; it is only a pity that the stories are mostly so banal and the books so ill-produced.

Storytelling is one of the most natural of human activities. We all do it. We come home from work and tell our partner what happened in the office, what the boss said and what she did and then this happened and what a catastrophe but that's not the end of it, there'll be more to come tomorrow since this is the days of our lives as soap opera. A child comes home from school and tells daddy a complicated story with immense gusto, sound effects, a concern for climax and a control of plot that is astonishing in anyone let alone so young. A little later, when mummy comes home and daddy says 'Tell mummy the story of the fish the lavatory and the stolen marbles', the child will look vacant, mumble something, and slope off. The story has been told, its narrative impulse has been obeyed, the teller is no longer interested.

As we get older we learn how to keep on telling the story of the fish and the stolen marbles, we polish it up, we alter it to make it work better. There weren't four people in the lavatory, there were fifteen. The fish wasn't a goldfish, it was an enormous great carp. When we tell this story, now become an anecdote, in public we do not want our loved ones to say, hang on, it wasn't quite like that. We know that what counts is the shape of the story, its impetus, its surprise value. Sticking to the facts may not be what it is about. We are all unreliable narrators when it comes to crafting good stories.

But we keep them carefully, we nurture them, we store them safely. When we make new friends or lovers we take them out of their safekeeping and offer them as a token of affection, a gift of love. We need to recognise that we are all storykeepers on an intimate level, and sometimes on a grander scale.

Families have their stories that they tell. Remember the picnic at the lagoon where Aunty Maude fell in and her wig got washed off. No, that wasn't the lagoon, it was the river and it was Aunty Lal who lost the wig. No, it wasn't, it was the dam and it wasn't a wig, it was a false bun. That was the time when the cows stood all over the picnic. No, that was when we went out on the lake in the rowing boat and lost the oars. There are as many different versions as there are relations, and they are all convinced their version is the true one.

If this happens in families, what about countries? Lucky ones have had myths and legends for a very long time, beyond remembering quite how or why, which exist in different versions but with a general consensus about the shapes of the narrative if not the detail. Constant telling has shaped them into a firm form which has the weight, not exactly of truth (Did Ulysses' men actually get turned into pigs? Did Minerva really spring fully formed from her father's head?) but of received wisdom. Of that paradoxical and ambiguous recounting that allows us to perceive not their truth but truths about our human nature.

Other countries have borrowed them in what now seems a quite mysterious but usefully bold way, as the English and indeed a number of European countries took over the myths of the Greeks and Romans and were quite happy to think about their lives in these arguably quite foreign terms. We can still call on Venus and Mars to try to make sense of our behaviour, Cupid is alive and well, Hermes not just a plush brand name. Christianity brought us the Bible with an immense wealth of stories. The Irish the Germans the Finns have their folktales. The English claim King Arthur.

And each country has its fairies, more or less sinister creatures who play variously damaging roles in people's lives. When I was young I wanted to live in a world peopled by these dangerously enchanting creatures. I knew a lot about them because the children's library allowed you to borrow only two books at a time, and one of them had to be non-fiction (bizarre rule) which was a chore for me until I discovered that fairy stories counted as non-fiction (even more bizarre, but maybe perceptive) and read everything I could find. They were often national in origin, which may have been why I thought my country should have some. So I wrote my own fairy stories, transferred to the local scenery. I called my little people Australian Bushelves, ABs for short. Not a catchy name, no wonder I never got them out into the world. There was a lot of native flora and fauna from the local Newcastle bush in these stories, but the ABs behaved like characters in an Enid Blyton adventure.

I was in fact putting my finger on a problem. What stories does our country offer us? There are things that, following our English heritage, we can shamelessly borrow. I may not consider myself a good Christian but I believe that the culture that religion created, Christendom, belongs to me. I may not go all the way with Norman Lindsay and Sidney Long, peopling gum tree glades with nymphs and satyrs, but I've got them quite comfortably in my head. Other borrowings are more difficult; we are still not sure what relationship we can have with the stories of indigenous Australians.

So, what of our stories? What belong to us, what have we made, what borrowed? How reliably do we quote and recount the past? How consciously should we reconstruct it?

At school I read widely, but not very Australianly. In my teens in still fairly nineteenth-century Newcastle I found more familiarity in the London of *The Forsyte Saga* than the outback. At university reading English honours we started with Beowulf and moved through Middle English to Chaucer and meticulously ticked off every century to the present, with forays into American and Irish literature. No Australian. Except for some poems of Alec Hope.

And he hardly counts in the Australian stakes, you might say. Ah: I think you would be entirely wrong. I think Hope is very much a poet of his native land, and I think to fail to see him as such is to make a sadly common mistake about what constitutes Australianness, and one that only recently was made by the judges of the Miles Franklin Award, who paid attention and that very narrowly only to content. Hope was a poet coming out of the traditions of Christendom, of Greek and Roman mythologies, but he wrote about this country and what it was like to live here and be a person trying to manage life here.

Once I talked to a group of university students in Halle, in Germany. What makes you an Australian writer? I was asked. A good question. Mainly, I said, the fact that I say I am. I could say that my sensibility was formed here but then I know a lot of good Australian writers whose sensibilities were formed quite elsewhere. Because I publish here? Publishing overseas wouldn't change my sense of who I am. Most claims can thus be doubted, all except the one, I am Australian because that is how I see myself.

I also want to see myself as heir to a tradition. Not a neat one, not one susceptible to strict taxonomies, but one whose watchwords are diversity and discreteness and multiplicity. Owing more to the ragbag than the file. You can lose things in files, if you forget what you filed them under. Ragbags are much safer. (For anybody too young to know what ragbags are, they are ad hoc receptacles in which thrifty people kept all the bits of stuff that might come in handy one day.) They are full of treasures. And every fragment tells a story.

Storykeepers is a rummage in that ragbag, prompted by the curiosity about the past that Federation fever has aroused. It is a recognition that to turn experience into story is to control it, to own it, and that to forget or to remain ignorant of our stories is to be doomed, possibly to repeat them, but perhaps worse, to lose them altogether. We have not always been as careful as we might have been.

To celebrate the hundred-year-old creation of a national entity from a noisily disparate set of parts might be a cause for congratulation, but that could after a while feel smug. To make it a matter for questioning is likely to be more edgy, more uneasy, and give rise to thinking rather than complacency.

Questions: that's how the process that ended in this collection of writing began, with the Word Festival, in Canberra. To celebrate its occurrence in Federation Centenary year it asked a number of them. Who are we? Where do we come from? Where are we going? What will become of us? What are we making of ourselves? Who says? Who cares? Writers visiting the festival addressed these questions, and a number of them were asked to write the pieces published here.

Their brief? It could be summed up in the phrase, living writers write about dead writers. To remind us that dead writers are not dead if their writings are still alive to us. Each of the people approached was asked to choose an Australian writer from the past who was interesting to them, and make a response to his or her work. The emphasis was to be as much on the response as on the original work. In other words, the contemporary writer was to be a character in the narrative, along with the dead one. The result could be a kind of conversation. The commission was to be considered in the broadest way desirable. Do what you like, I said. Use your imagination however you wish.

The results, in two poems, one story and a variety of essays, would need some pretty procrustean editorial lopping in some cases, and a creatively biased reading or indeed misreading, in others, to fit the brief. Some do without any help. But what they all do is fit the title, which came last in the process, and was indeed inspired by the way in which they all so fascinatingly explored some variation of the themes the name *Storykeepers* offers.

The notion of stories and storytelling has been ubiquitous in this Federation year. There's something of a *Zeitgeist* about it. It is a significant element in the National Museum of Australia's opening exhibitions, and the National Library's publication about its Treasures is called *Telling Australia's Stories*. But I wanted something more than the idea of story-telling, which may be a benign and charming process; I wanted to make a stronger statement about what was or should be or wasn't happening.

That is where the idea of storykeeping comes in. It makes us aware that stories are things that exist, that must be found, that must be preserved and guarded, with respect, not stolen or usurped or rewritten. That they are fragile, and may sift away into a fine powdery dust, or fragment into unrecognisable shards, or like the paper they are written on, fade under bright light. They must be saved from perishing.

The word *keep* is astonishingly various in its applications. We keep house. We keep faith, we keep track, tabs, time, step, the peace. We keep in touch. We keep the flame. The home fires burning and the wolf from the door. We keep abreast, away, fit, from, going, we keep in and keep out, we keep up (in a number of ways), we keep company. We keep awake, keep mum, in the dark. We keep tight. We keep safe. We keep in the sense of catching and imprisoning. We keep records, we keep tally. We keep watch and ward. We keep alive. We keep quiet, private, secret. And them we fail to keep, in a whole lot of negatives of the process; we lose. We have allowed and even delighted in loss, theft, destruction.

And consider the noun, the thing that is kept, the keepsake. Plenty of those to remind us of what we have saved, and what we have lost. The National Museum, which provides the images for the book, is full of them, in all their idiosyncratic poignancy.

And then there are jolly little jingles. *Finders keepers*, our forebears might have chanted, as they told themselves the country was terra nullius. *Losers weepers*. The indigenous inhabitants still feel the truth of that.

There are gatekeepers, keeping in, keeping out. I'd like to think that this collection does not claim such a role. Fishing treasures out of the ragbag is a matter of serendipity, not policing.

Putting together such a collection of writing is a curious

business. You believe in it, otherwise why would you do it? But somehow, when it happens, it is astonishing. This one was, twice over. Because I had no idea what fine things would turn up. And I had no idea that they would relate to one another so engagedly. It is quite mysterious, the accidental nature of a collection like this. You decide who you want to have in it, some people say yes but others say no, and then afterwards you think of wonderful writers that you wished you'd remembered to ask. So there are lots of ways in which it is accidental, even arbitrary.

And then the pieces start coming in and you realise they are talking to one another. A good collection is a conversation. First a dialogue starts among the pieces, and then readers are invited in. It's like getting in a bunch of people for a party, simply because you like them, and discovering that they all get along famously. There's a good buzz to it.

It's interesting that a number of the living writers asked to pay attention to dead ones chose to talk about people who actually never did write at all because they never got the chance to, whose voices were stolen, or muted, who had stories to tell but didn't because they were rendered dumb by a society that turned deaf ears upon them. Who had things to say, knowledge to give, wisdom to impart, but were not listened to.

We tell one another stories in order to learn how to live. Unless our stories are kept we will perish. There is a hierarchy to it, a sense of passing down, from elders to youngers, and also an awareness that some have special gifts for this sort of thing.

Alexis Wright's memoir of her grandmother is called 'Don't Say Anything', and begins with a reiteration of those words. They are special words, and when spoken by senior relatives have the force of law. Family members are bidden to keep silent, in order to keep the peace. Keep quiet, keep mum, keep your head down. That way you keep safe.

The grandmother could not read or write, but she grew flowers, and vegetables, fruits and trees. She cultivated her garden, and her life. And she told stories: she was the keeper of the family stories. Alexis is rescuing the narrative of her life, she is making sure we keep her in mind. A simple woman, ordinary, as most of our grandmothers were, and yet extraordinary too, in her endurance, which is another kind of keeping: keeping on.

There is keeping quiet, and there is being kept quiet. There are a number of voices, lost or stolen, remembered in this book. There are children who did not grow up, women whose lives were cut off, emblematic stories of white destruction of black civilisation. As well as white celebrations of black civilisations, stories written with love as well as anger. There are masterpieces lost that ought to be retrieved, and histories mislaid that have been found again. Some stories however black keep from despair. Others keep memories alive. 'Memoir,' says Peter Goldsworthy, 'is an act of conservation.' Some are fearful indictments of the carelessness, the failure to keep or even to see that there were essential things to be kept, that seemed to lose a whole race. Remembering is offered as counter to dismembering.

The word housekeeping has lost a lot of its force in current wranglings over who in a partnership should do the housework, but if you pay attention you can hear a kind of biblical import in it. And when you expand it into the phrase, keeping your house in order, it has considerable metaphorical weight. Many of these accounts are ways of desiring to find and to keep a fruitful order in the society, the house, we live in.

A number of the writers in this book make the discovery that there can be an astonishing modernity in thinking on the part of our forebears. And that to stereotype them is to diminish ourselves. And that when we think we are inventing something it may be because we have forgotten that somebody long ago thought of it.

Some contributors offer meditations on writing, which are tributes from one craftsman to another. There are records kept of life and death. There is a quietness which listens to the past speaking to the present. And there is an idea of the – perhaps slightly surprising – company which writers should be seen to keep.

The last piece shows us how a reading of current politics in the context of Henry Lawson's examination in his fictions of what it is to be Australian, 'what Australia – that place and that idea for which he wrote "with all his heart" – actually means', can illuminate the way we see ourselves today …. Who are we … where are we going … who cares?

There may be some answers to these questions in the pieces collected here. But I don't think that is the important thing. The important thing is to keep asking them. To keep paying attention. To keep in mind the past that brought us to this moment. The central shining thread of *Storykeepers* is its keeping faith with a history not always comfortable but nonetheless belonging to us. If we are familiar with our stories we may be able to change the plot, perhaps, produce a happy ending, help the good triumph; at the very least we may experience the catharsis that a powerful narrative offers.

The book will I hope be a reminder, in the personal and idiosyncratic terms of a fairly random number of clear-sighted contemporary writers, of the predecessors and forebears who began this job of giving us words in which to find ourselves.

Marion Halligan
2000

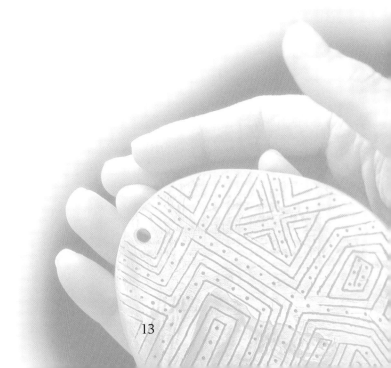

gary crew

THEIR GHOSTS MAY BE HEARD:

A RESPONSE TO ERNEST FAVENC'S

NOVEL *MAROONED IN AUSTRALIA*

THE CELEBRATED DUTCH VESSEL *Batavia* was wrecked on the Abrolhos Islands, off the Western Australian Coast, on 4 June 1629. More than 120 men, women and children met their deaths in the massacre that followed as tragically, having survived the shipwreck, passengers and crew turned against each other with unspeakable violence. Jan Pelgrom (aged seventeen) and Wouter Loos (aged about thirty) – although found guilty of participating in these murders – were spared death and cast away on the mainland of Terra

Australis Incognita. Thus, almost 150 years before Cook had even sighted the continent, Loos and Pelgrom had already become – as best we know – the first European inhabitants of Australia.

I was born in Queensland in 1947 and throughout my school-days the wall map of the British Empire still showed India as blood red despite that nation's hard-won independence. And so, I suppose, with such obvious gaps in my education (were they purposefully engineered?) it should come as no surprise that I had never heard of the *Batavia*, let alone the wreck and massacre, nor the landing of any Europeans prior to Cook.

After having taken the well-worn path of a Queensland working-class boy through the 1940s to 60s I left school at Year 10 to work as a cadet draftsman. After ten years at that, and hating every minute, I re-educated myself by enrolling in Arts at the University of Queensland in 1973. It was there that I met the progressive Dr Helen Tiffin and soon fell in love with what was known as 'Post Colonial Fiction' – or, as some called the new subject – 'The Empire Writes Back'!

To my amazement I found that indigenous peoples of declining European Empires worldwide could not only speak the Queen's English (Forgive my ignorance. After all, I did but see her passing by, as an earlier Australian luminary had already gushed.) but they had actually employed that language to write poetry and plays and novels and histories and …

It was through this literature, most often written back to the invader in English, that I began to understand the essential

catastrophe of Colonisation. Stated plainly, when the invader/
coloniser took over – whether Dutch, British, Portuguese,
Spanish, whoever – they attempted to destroy everything: the
land, the culture, the humanity and spirituality of these peoples and yes, even their history.

Often horrified, always learning, I read and read.

After completing my Masters in Literature, I became an
English teacher and (naturally) began a novel. I chose to
'*Reconstruct the life of a young castaway abandoned on this con-
tinent before white settlement*'.

Those words are taken directly from my writer's journal
dated 11 July 1988. I decided to base this novel on the outcomes of the wreck of the *Batavia*, alluding to the terrible
massacre that followed, but concentrating on the fate of the
two Dutch males, Pelgrom and Loos, (one hardly more than a
boy – his testosterone levels probably raging) dumped here as
punishment and never heard of again.

Well. Not quite. As you will see …

Being a teacher, I wanted to keep in touch with my youth
audience but also give this book a 'Post-Colonial, Post-
Structural' adult readership edge.

My reasoning was simple. I had learned that History
defied every human attempt to set it in stone: that History
slipped and slithered, demanding new interpretations with
every new bone found, every new document discovered.

My somewhat bizarre and ambitious project was given
the nod by my publisher Ron Norman, of William Heinemann
Publishers – who just happened to be a Jamaican – and away I

went on the fabulous research adventure that led me to write *Strange Objects*.

The literary tradition of 'shipwreck and castaway stories' (and those castaways' association with indigenous peoples) had begun with Defoe's *Robinson Crusoe* and Swift's *Gulliver's Travels*.

As European Empires expanded, so too did the demand for books that suited the prevalent taste in Colonial Conquest, especially those associated with the adventures and horrors of shipwrecks – and encounters with 'cannibals'. Indeed, there seemed to be cannibals on every island in the Southern Hemisphere – though if the truth were known, as it is becoming more and more so – a shipwrecked European sailor was far more likely to be eaten by his own than his islander Brothers.

This shipwreck/castaway genre was exploited in the very best 'Nice shot that!' British fashion by R.M. Ballantyne in *The Coral Island* and continued merrily (or should I say *brutally* and *self-righteously?*) on its way through the nineteenth century to spawn such remarkable novels as Conrad Sayce's *The Splendid Savage: A Tale of the North Coast of Australia* in which one white castaway youth, having mistaken another for a 'savage', soon learns that he is one of his own.

In a distinctly homoerotic – and horribly racist – scene, the 'splendid savage' (who turns out to be no more than a well-tanned European castaway from a previous shipwreck) is described by the young fellow who discovers him as:

Over six feet tall, broad, and of magnificent proportions. His only dress was a peculiar short skirt like two aprons of soft skin hanging in front and behind, leaving his powerful legs free play. I thought his skin was black at first, as he came closer I saw that I was wrong: it was a beautiful deep brown … This wonderful specimen of manhood halted a few yards from me and looked straight at me. His face was in keeping with his body: a high, intelligent forehead, big piercing eyes set well apart, nose, lips, and chin denoting high breeding and great courage. This was no Australian blackfellow. Never, even in pictures of Greek athletes, had I seen such a perfect man.

I had no desire to satirise this 'shipwreck/castaway' genre that William Golding had already so splendidly savaged in his *The Lord of the Flies*.

Besides, there was yet another colonial literary tradition, what might well be called the 'Boys' Own Fiction' genre. This second genre was often prefaced by the author as being written to suit 'boys aged from nine to ninety'.

This could be aptly named the 'Peter Pan Syndrome', representing the Victorian/Edwardian man-boy who would never grow up and for whom 'to die was the greatest adventure'. I wonder if the brutalised and dying indigenous boys (dare I say, 'The Lost Boys'?) believed that? How ignorant and arrogant. In fact, how utterly imperial!

The basis of this 'Boys' Own' genre was the inland exploration adventure novel after Rider Haggard and Conan Doyle.

In these stories, usually aimed at both men and the ubiquitous boy-man, a party of male Europeans (led by a 'civilised' and benign indigene who speaks the Mother Tongue in an 'amusing' way) discover a new, or lost civilisation, often arising from ancient European antecedents. As the real genesis of this civilisation is European (spawned by some long lost and earlier expedition of Europeans) the new and hybrid race (often sterile) is always depicted as being superior to that of the 'savage' indigenes.

It is typical of this genre that the superior race (that is, the newly created hybrid) had usually attempted to educate and 'enlighten' the indigenous people then, deeming them too ignorant and untrustworthy – or not worth the effort to 'save' – brutalised and demeaned them to the level of slaves.

As these 'discovered' civilisations were also generally located in exotic places, they were often rich in gold or precious stones. Of course, being Christians and not remotely interested in material wealth, the second wave of Europeans, that is, the explorers who found (read: *stumbled upon*) the new civilisation, initially declared that they wanted none of this wealth, but always managed to take some home.

Ironically, before they departed, the new wave explorers/ colonisers also managed to do two other things: they invariably succeeded in destroying, or being privy to, the destruction of both the original native race and the newly created hybrid civilisation.

Well done, lads!

Rather than visit these awful spaces again, I wanted to

create a text that questioned the very nature of how History is constructed. Given that nobody knows (to date, at least) what actually became of those castaways of the *Batavia*: the boy, Jan Pelgrom, and his adult offsider, Wouter Loos, I had open slather. Governed by research of course …

I read all that I could on the subject of the Dutch East India Company (the VOC), Dutch investigations of the western coast of Terra Australis en route to Jakarta (then known as Batavia), the *Batavia* itself and the recent maritime archaeology on the wreck. Quite a few scholars and authors had already done their homework on this, notably: Henrietta Drake Brockman in *Voyage to Disaster* which contains an English translation of Commander Francisco Pelsaert's journal of the wreck and its aftermath which led to Pelgrom and Loos being cast away. I also used Hugh Edwards' *The Wreck on Halfmoon Reef* and many others have since been published.

I learned a great deal, but few authors or scholars had attempted to actually research or reconstruct what had become of the two castaways once they were abandoned on the continent. Nearly all research centred on what happened on the islands – including the wreck itself and the massacre which followed.

I was delighted.

Using research on castaways from general fiction and non-fiction I began to build my story through my journal. I decided to dispense with the actual shipwreck as fast as I could, get off the island, and explore what might have become of the castaways.

But I needed a grab. A fictional 'in' to seduce my reader and yet simultaneously set up the 'what is the nature of History?' theme of my narrative. Since the events of the massacre on the Abrolhos had been so horrific, I researched similar events from both the past and present. I looked into issues such as cult suicide and the concept of *folie à deux* where hysteria had swept through a cult leading to violent outcomes. The nuns of Loudon came to mind. The Jamestown mass suicides. Waco.

Such readings helped me understand what might have precipitated the murders following the wreck of the *Batavia*, but none were any help in providing me with the 'narrative hook' I was looking for. And then I remembered a truly worthy non-fiction title, Stephen King's *Danse Macabre* with its analysis of the horror genre and its 'Tales of the Hook'. As a result, I opened *Strange Objects* with two modern literature grabs: the first a quote from H.P. Lovecraft:

> For there are strange objects in the great abyss, and the dreamer of dreams must take care not to stir up, or meet, the wrong ones …

And the second, a classic horror device used by King: the introduction of an urban myth hitch-hiking serial killer.

By now, certain purists may think that I am a total literary prostitute, or some sort of low life literary philistine. I don't think so. History is a curious concept. As I have said, it is hard to pin down. In fact, History is a living and evolving concept, not graven in the foundation stones of museums any more than it is to be found stored in the ivory towers of academia. No. Since History is composed of, or constructed upon, the actions and reactions of human beings, it is a composite of all elements of life: the beautiful, the horrific, the imagined, the real, and the fact that the imagination IS real. If that is not true, writers would not write.

Think about it ...

So I wanted to write a book to demonstrate this conundrum. This confusion. This glorious thing called History ... A book that used a non-linear, multi-genre structure to look at how History is a living concept – alive and multifaceted. Even more so, multi-*interpretive*.

I must have done something right. First published in 1990, *Strange Objects* took off from Day One and hasn't landed yet. It has won many awards both in Australia and overseas and, to my delight, is constantly evolving in readership and usage – both in age and purpose. It has been published as both an Adult novel and a Young Adult novel without one word being changed.

A curious evolution. Like History, even.

But ... (it wouldn't be narrative if there wasn't a but ...!), in 1998, eight years after *Objects* was first published, while reading Maurice Saxby's *Offered to Children: A History of Australian Children's Literature 1841–1941*, I came across a reference to an author I had never heard of: Ernest Favenc.

Saxby's work had compared Favenc's 1896 novel,

Marooned on Australia; Being the Narration of Diedrich Buys of his Discoveries and Exploits in Terra Australis Incognita about the year 1630 to my *Strange Objects*.

How had I missed Favenc in my research?

In his text, Saxby explained that the Favenc novel was loosely based on the fate of the two *Batavia* castaways and then, to my utter amazement, I read:

> [Favenc's novel] was a move away from the well-worn
> adventure trail … More significantly, Favenc explores
> the psychological tension between Diedrich and Paul
> {the second castaway} and their opposing character traits
> … A significance that was to be reworked by Gary Crew
> almost one hundred years later in his novel *Strange
> Objects*.

After I had popped a couple of Valium and downed a few brandies, I found the courage to ring Maurie and ask him about the similarities between the books.

'Don't stress,' he assured me. 'Your books are nothing alike. Besides Favenc's is well and truly out of print.'

I felt a bit better, though still sullied. Even guilty. So I set about an archival search for Favenc's book. When I found it, I felt *much* better. Oh sure there were similarities. Uncanny similarities. But vast differences too.

Although Favenc and I had used the wreck of the *Batavia* as our stated base, he had fictionalised the names of the castaways, while keeping their ages reasonably accurate: Diedrich

Buys being the younger (about eighteen) and Paul, the 'Wouter Loos' character being much older than history suggests. We had both cut straight to the chase and left out most of the psycho-drama of the wreck and the massacre on the Abrolhos. Curiously we both also used the personal journal format to tell the castaways' story – although Favenc had chosen to make his narrator the younger of the two (Diedrich Buys) while I chose the older (Wouter Loos). I felt that this was more likely as the Pelgrom/Buys youth was little more than an ignorant cabin boy on the *Batavia* and probably could neither read nor write. The Loos/Paul character, on the other hand, had conducted such a powerful self defence that Pelsaert had allowed him to live while the boy had escaped execution purely on the premise of his youth, not his persuasive language skills.

Perhaps (like me) Favenc was wanting two bites of the publishing apple in using the younger narrator to appeal to both a youth and adult audience too. I mean, my hitch-hiker narrative hook was introduced as part of the journal of Steven Messenger, a modern teenage sociopath and, throughout *Strange Objects* this motif runs parallel to the journal of Wouter Loos written three hundred years earlier.

Further, both Favenc and I had set the two castaways against one another almost immediately, which presented another interesting outcome: since only one member of the pair wrote the journal, what evidence was there that *his* version was not personally biased in favour of his own 'rightness' or even 'self-righteousness'? Under these circumstances, our readers are left with yet another conundrum: could there be a genuine journal (both actual AND factual) written by one of the castaways still waiting to be found in the Western Australian desert and presenting yet another version of this 'History'?

Mind you, it might not be the truth either.

Favenc used footnotes throughout his text to add to its verisimilitude. So did I. In both cases, some of references are true; some are false.

For example, Favenc quite rightly notes that '[Abel] Tasman was instructed ... to endeavour to find the two men left by Pelsa[e]rt'. I noted this too. But then, Favenc's discovery of a 'Latin Missal inside of which I could trace in faded characters: *Jean Binot Paulmier de Gonneville. Honfleur, 1503*', is almost certainly a fabrication.

Although there is reference to an alleged visit of the explorer de Gonneville to Australia at about the time stated by Favenc, this remains unsubstantiated. Flavenc sets up his Haggardesque 'lost white civilisation' using surviving crew members of the wreck of de Gonneville's ship as its progenitors.

Curiously, in *Objects*, I had drawn upon the historically verified wreck of the British vessel *Tryal* (wrecked 1622: site discovered 1969) to produce my earlier European contact, constructing from that wreck the fiction of the girl Ela, who supposedly survived the *Tryal* and wandered down Aboriginal trade routes to finally meet her nemesis at the hands of the white castaway, Pelgrom.

Following the 'Lost Kingdom' genre of his time, Favenc

has his wandering castaways discover the fully developed 'European caste' city of de Gonneville's offspring. Having chosen not to use the 'new civilisation' motif, I did not have any references to alien civilisation or architecture yet, both Flavenc and I did use rock art of varying forms. He used authentic reference to Grey's discovery of Aboriginal *Wandjina* art. I used the simplistic child art of Ela (etched into a cave wall in a naïve style, using a technique reminiscent of traditional Aboriginal rock pecking) to provide an enduring and symbolic visual interpretation of the physical characteristics and sexual potency of my castaways.

We both used the lure of riches. Favenc based his on the discovery of gold; I used the device that Loos mistook great lumps of quartz crystal for diamonds.

Obviously we both knew that the Dutch, like all colonists, were in it for the money.

One of the principal differences between our narratives is that Favenc's takes place entirely in the past while mine flexes from the past to the present. This 'time flexing' is a deliberate device to ensure that History is seen as 'The Eternal Present', not a thing that has been and gone and can now be dissected, like a corpse or a fossil. I therefore deliberately gave the discovery of Wouter Loos' journal to the modern youth, Steven Messenger. He finds it in an iron pot on a Biology Excursion. This vessel (dumped from the wreck because it was too heavy to warrant carrying back to Batavia Town following rescue) sealed by dust and age, is immediately labelled by the media as 'the cannibal pot', as it contains a human hand still wearing a gold ring. This is in fact the hand of the white girl Ela, (respectfully mummified by her adoptive Aboriginal associates) and preserved in the pot by one of the castaways.

Both Loos and Pelgrom vanished. Their ultimate ending is unclear. Perhaps Loos disappears into the interior in search of the fabled 'diamonds' of his diseased and capitalistic imagination (or simply read *greed*). Pelgrom, the more evil of the pair, apparently metamorphoses into the persona of the future Colonisers, (read *murderers, pillagers and rapists*) to reappear as Steven Messenger … and very possibly the ubiquitous 'Hitch Hiker' murderer.

Favenc, however, chose a more 'neatly tied off' narrative for his castaways. Paul destroys the 'pseudo-European' civilisation and pays the ultimate price, while the second, and younger, Diedrich Buys, returns to Holland (and becomes very wealthy) thus bringing his journal to a close. However, in *Strange Objects* the journal of Wouter Loos lives on via human contact and (mis)interpretation through its modern discoverer, Steven Messenger and the unresolved outcomes of the fate of the ring found on the mummified hand. In other words, the History of *Strange Objects* (hopefully) is neither locked up, nor dead, but lives in the non-resolution of the tale.

For all of the literary tricks employed by both Favenc and myself in re-creating the lives of the castaways of the *Batavia*, far more than our words live on …

In 1994 I found an amazing book entitled *And Their Ghosts May Be Heard* in which author/scholar Rupert Gerritsen postulates that, after a study of the contemporary Aboriginal peoples of the Murchison River Basin (inland from the Abrol-hos) there is clear evidence of white genetic, linguistic and cultural incursion. That is, 'living evidence' of survivors of a European wreck remains with us.

And so, whether through *Strange Objects* or *Marooned on Australia* or possibly through the genes of the castaways of the *Batavia*, History lives on … and not only in the ghostly realm of fiction.

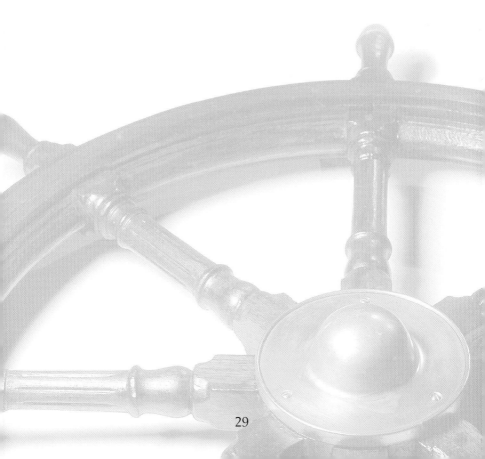

greg dening

READING TO WRITE

THE PAST I VISIT – the two-hundred-year past that I
visit – is on paper. Mostly. Sometimes it is in things with
human creativity encapsulated in them – machinery, ornament,
art, buildings, landscape. A two-hundred-year past is beyond
experience and memory, though. And beyond the radar of our
various electronic recording systems. There are no voices from
two hundred years ago, no smells, no touches, no movement.

No, the two-hundred-years past I visit is stilled onto
paper, millions of pieces of paper. Written-on paper. One-off
pieces of paper, mostly without copy. Not printed paper.
Handwritten paper. Script. The first mark of my history is

always a pen's or a pencil's. The first mark of my history, the first readings I make, are always shaped by the transience of the moment in which they were made. The hand that writes them is still trembling with anger or fear or sorrow. Or it is scribbled in a hurry. Or it is flourished with power. It is stained or burnt on its edges, or blotted. It is corrected and erased. It belongs to times that are as long or short or broken or continuous as the human experience that sustains it.

To visit my two-hundred-year past, I read and look. I read to write. No, actually, I read to live; reading for me is life. I love the dance on the beaches of the mind that reading is. I read fast and slow. I love the slow reading of a poem. Better still, I love to hear the slow reading of a poem. I slow read the sacred texts in my life. I soak up the timelessness of their words. These sacred texts look like they are bound to time but they are not. Their meaning stretches out to me beyond the meaning their writers ever had. I easily fly over their contradictions and errors and know what truth they hold for me.

I read fast most of the time. That is because reading books, as distinct from the written-on pages of my two-hundred-year past – reading-books is my conversation with the world. My eyes are ahead of my mind when I read fast. I gobble sentences, paragraphs, pages whole. There is a white noise in the back of my mind as I read. It is the babble of worldwide conversations that affect my thinking. I'm in conversation with novelists, philosophers, anthropologists, historians, critics in this sort of reading. It is full of erotic, ecstatic moments when I think that what they are saying is what I myself am just about to say. But I'm going to say it better!

So I agree with a thinker like Michel de Certeau, a writer who makes such challenging reflections on *The Practice of Everyday Life*.

Reading, in his view, is a creative act 'full of detours and drifts across the page, imaginary or meditative flights taking off from a few words, overlapping paragraph on paragraph, page on page, shortlived dances of the eye and mind'.

Reading for me is also pro-active, creative. It is in no way passive, a mirror to someone else's thoughts. My eyes might be attached to the page, but my mind is soaring.

That is reading books. When I read my one-off pieces of paper in script, it is somewhat different. I would like to show you how.

I read to write true stories, history. All stories need to be true, perhaps you will say. Stories need to be honest to the realities of living, experiential, recognisably human. Even the most maverick, bizarre or eccentric behaviour has to be recognisably human. Stories don't need to be specifically accurate, but they need to be generically true.

My true stories are something else. There is a heavy obligation that I owe the past. If I claim to represent it – if I claim to re-present it – I owe it its own independence. Whatever happened in the past happened with its own uniqueness of time and space. Much that characterises what happens might be repeated in the generic way of all stories, but the uniqueness of all the things that come together to make its present moment is total. It is unrepeatable as it happened. If I intrude on the past, I owe it a gift of itself. The history I write will always be mine and something more than the past, but there is a part of it that is never mine. It is the part that actually happened, independently of my knowing that or how it happened. My true stories are ruled by my belief that I have always something to learn.

I read to write. I write to give back to the past its own present moments. There is no better place to catch that tenuous, trembling moment than when the pen is first put to paper. I am a pilgrim and initiate when I want to read that piece of paper. That piece of paper never comes to me like a book does. I must go to it where it is housed. Wherever it is housed, it is cared for. It is precious, and there are rules to be obeyed to read it – gloves to be put on, pencils to be used rather than ink, logs to be signed in and out, silence to be kept.

Wherever it is done, reading the written-down past is special. It is as creative as the ordinary reading of books, but there is something more. My eye must travel from the word on the page up the pen and hand and into the person of the writer. That word on the page has a past and a history, it is not just born there and then, but it doesn't yet have its future. I, the historian two hundred years on, might think that I know the future and consequences of that word. But the writer doesn't. The present moment for the writer is full of ambiguity. My stories to be true must catch that ambiguity.

Enough of abstractions and reflections. Let me read to write a true story.

He is subject to violent perspiration & particularly in his hands so that he soils anything he handles.

These were the worst moments of his life. He stands barefoot and dishevelled in the stern of the launch, the object of curses and screams of hatred from the deck of the *Bounty* above. His decisive moment has come. William Bligh must reconcile himself to the fact of his mutiny. He must order the painter to be cut, lest the *Bounty* drag the launch under, and before the threats of murder become reality.

The faces of the eighteen men in the launch now turn to him. They are in the middle of a vast ocean with six or seven inches of way in the overloaded launch. There is sullen anger on the faces too. Nearly all of them blame him for the situation they are in. He stares back suspiciously at them. His paranoia is as close to the surface of his person as it ever is. He cannot understand how all this could have happened to him without the men in the launch knowing.

They look back at the *Bounty* and see young Tom Ellison scamper to the shrouds and loosen the sails to set her on a north-west-west tack. Their memory of the sprightly way Ellison performed an act so wanton of their lives would one day be his death sentence. Tom Ellison would be one of only three who would be hanged for the mutiny on the *Bounty*.

Bligh thinks he hears at that moment a shout from the *Bounty*, 'Huzzah for Otaheite'. He is the only one who hears it. Perhaps that is because he is already fashioning in his mind a history of the events that have changed his life so drastically.

It was about 9.00 in the morning of 29 April 1789 (calendar time: in ship's time days begin at noon: in ship's time it was 9.00am 28 April). The night before from the decks of the *Bounty* they had seen the fires of the volcano on Tofua island, one of the Tongan group. This morning they can see its steam column beyond the horizon. They start to row towards it. It is fifty miles away.

No sooner are they on their way than Bligh asks for pen and paper. He also asks if there is anyone among them who has a log or journal. Peter Hayward produces a small pocketbook. He had used three pages of it to note his captain's instructions on the signals he should use when he was in charge of the *Bounty*'s boats. It has 108, 160 x 100mm pages that Bligh can use. We have that pocketbook still. It was literally Bligh's bosom companion for the forty-two days and 3700 nautical miles of their voyage. Bligh writes daily notes in it, makes his navigational calculations, draws and surveys the islands they pass and discover. When weather permits it, he transcribes and enlarges his notes in the *Bounty*'s log which he had made sure to secure. His passion is to put everything that had happened to him on paper. He is unsure whether he will survive. He is certain that he cannot trust those with him to tell his story as he wants. He denies them any paper to record their own thoughts.

We have this water-stained, cluttered pocketbook still. It is one of the most extraordinary pieces of paper from which I have ever written true stories.

Bligh's first entry reads:

28 April 1789
Just before Sun Rise the People mutinied Seized me while
asleep in my Cabbin tied my Hands behind my back and
carried me on Deck in my Shirt. Put 18 of the crew into the
launch and me after them and set us a drift – Tofoa bear-
ing NE 10 leag^s – Ship steered to NNW – four cutlasses
were thrown into the Boat

Then on three loose leaves, back and front, he begins a description of the twenty-five 'pirates' who had taken his ship. He
questions those in the launch about the pirates' distinguishing
marks. He knows the Navy will search the ends of the earth to
find them.

All of them are tattooed. Tattoo is a Polynesian word. A
tattoo was a South Seas souvenir for a sailor. A group of them
have a star tattooed on their breast. It is their Order of the
Garter. James Morrison drives the point home. He has a garter
inscribed on his left leg inscribed with *Honi soit qui mal y
pense.* The youngest of them, Thomas Ellison, has his name tattooed on his right arm and *October 25 1788.* It is the date of
their first sighting of Tahiti. It was a birthday of a sort, but a
doomsday as well. He would celebrate on only two anniver-
saries of it before he was hanged.

Listen to Bligh's description of Fletcher Christian and
hear the passion in it.

*Fletcher Christian. Aged 24 Years – 5 feet. 9 In High
Dark Swarthy Complexion*

Complexion	*Dark & very swarthy*
Hair	*Blackish or very dark brown*
Make	*Strong*
Marks	*Star tatowed on the left breast and tatowed*

*on the backside. – His knees stands a little out and may
be called a little bow legged. He is subject to violent
perspiration & particularly in His hands so that he soils
anything he handles.*

It was a long day's row to Tofua. It would be too dark and the
waters too dangerous for them to land on its rocky shore. They
would spend the night in the launch. By morning it was blowing a gale. At the end of that terrible day, Bligh serves them *a
Morsel of Bread and a Gill of wine for each Person for dinner.*
They had five days' provisions. They didn't know then but
these provisions would have to last them forty-two days.

They had come to Tofua because it was handily there,
with no plan other than to survive and perhaps supplement
their provisions. But Tofua is volcanic barren. They can only
gather a few coconuts. They can barely stay on the rolled stone
beach for mosquitos. Bligh endures the mosquitos for two days
in a cave writing his papers.

By the second day they had been sighted by the natives of
the neighbouring island of Nomuka. Two hundred of them
collected in their canoes. Among them a young man recognised Bligh who had been on Nomuka with Cook on Cook's

last voyage. Nomukans had no love of these strangers. Cook had been at his violent worst, lopping ears, shaving heads, flogging, taking hostages.

It is not long before Bligh knows they cannot stay at Tofua. He hears the clacking of stones. It was something he had heard in Hawai'i after Cook's death, just before an attack.

Sunday May 3
Fresh Gales ESE to NE The Natives in great number prepared to attack us – I ordered all the People & what we had into the Boat – When in, I followed & the Natives began their attack Killed poor Norton – followed us in Cannoes – maimed us very much – rowed out to Sea – and after supplication from People at 8 at Night bore away for Timor after prayers, agreeing to live on a Gill of water & morsel of Bread our Stock of Provisions about 150lbs Bread 28 galls. Water 20lbs Pork 3 Bottles of Wine & 5 Quts Rum The difference from our first quantity owing to loss – a few Coconutts & some Breadfruit were in the Boat but the Latter useless. – divided into 2 watches & set a reefed lug foresail – at 8 am it blew a mere storm & and were in very eminant Danger – always bailing & in a horrible situation. Served a teaspoonful of Rum to each Person for we were very wet & Cold – at Noon latd 19° 27'S 182.52 E

Their days grew worse –

Saturday May 9 1789
Served a Gill of Water and ¹/₂ oz of Bread for Supper.
Sang a Song & went to Sleep.

After their Tofua experience, they dared not land. Bligh runs for the northern coast of New Holland and its Barrier Reef. They are wet all the time. They are bailing all the time. The sea is threatening to engulf them always. The twelve men not on watch had to lie for eight hours on the bottom of the boat so that the six on watch could work her.

For 23 May, the pocketbook reads:

Sea breaking all over us – constantly Bailing Have past a dread night with the Cold & Wet – Not a dry Thread

Sometime later, he translated these notes into his log:

May 23. The miseries of this day have exceeded the preceding. The night was dreadful. The sea flew over us with great forces and kept us bailing with horror and anxiety. At dawn of day I found everyone in a most distressed situation and now I began to fear another such night would produce the end of several who were no longer able to bear it.

Three weeks and a day into their voyage, they sight high land. It is New Holland. In the night they hear breakers on the reef.

Providentially, Bligh notes, they find a passage through the reef to smooth deep water. They make for a small island. Bligh calls it Restoration Island. It is the anniversary of King Charles II's restoration to the throne. Bligh adds: *It's a name not inapplicable to my present situation.*

There is no exuberance in their landing. They all know how far they still have to go. They stagger onto the small half-moon beach. The first thing they see is the skeleton of an eight-foot snake hanging over a branch. There are signs that natives visit the island, and kangaroos. They see some natives hallooing at them on the mainland. There is food – oysters and periwinkles and some edible vegetation. They have a pot, and Bligh's reading glass makes them a fire. The pain in their shrivelled, constipated bodies is constant. They are sullen and divided. Half of them sleep in the boat that night, half on the shore. In the night, the gudgeon – the metal plate that holds the eye of the rudder – falls off and is lost. It is an accident that shakes Bligh. Next day he retreats to a shady spot under a tree. He is there all day alone. Hallett brings him food. They think he is still with his papers and his maps. The pocketbook is full of his navigational calculations and sketch maps and coastal profiles. Navigation is his triumph – he is out by only 19 minutes longitude by modern satellite mapping. It is his command that is his disaster.

He is not navigating or indeed filling his log. He is composing a prayer:

It is full of thanksgiving and sorrow for sin, and promises never to forget mercies and to obey commandments. It is a composite from the Book of Common Prayer. It is all 'We' and 'us'. He stumbles only once into the singular:

> ... *Continue O Lord we beseech thee, through the media-*
> *tion of our blessed Saviour Jesus Christ, this thy goodness*
> *towards us, – strengthen my mind & guide our Steps –*
> *Grant unto us health and strength to continue our voyage,*
> *& and so bless our miserable morsel of Bread, that it may*
> *be sufficient for our undertaking ...*

They might have seemed safe within the reef, and they were – from the horrors of their open-sea voyaging. But they were no longer safe from themselves. Their hatreds ate at them. When they reached Sunday Island – round Cape York and into Torres Strait – it boiled over.

Bligh, the whole of the *Bounty*'s voyage, had been consumed with its importance. Nothing enraged him more than any seeming lack of altruism on the part of the crew towards its high purposes. And no-one enraged him more than William Purcell, the carpenter, whose capital in life was his tools and his skills. He saw little need to expend them unduly to the service of Bligh's high ambitions.

Everything that had gone on before in the bad relations of Purcell and Bligh came to a head on Sunday Island. Bligh found Purcell insolent to a high degree when Purcell suggested in so many words that he was as good a man as Bligh. It concerned some issue over sharing oysters that they had found. Bligh in a rage takes up a cutlass and orders Purcell to defend himself. It was as bizarre a place for a duel as there ever was. It was as ugly, in their circumstances, as it was laughable. John Fryer, the master, threatens to arrest them both. It is not something that any of them will forget.

The pocketbook has nothing of all this. The journal does.

I was determined to strike a formal blow, and either to preserve my command or die in the attempt … Some had totally forgot every degree of obedience. I saw no one openly scouting the offenders altho they were known … I now took a cutlass determined never to have it from under my seat or out of my reach, as providence had seemed pleased to give me sufficient strength to make use of it. I did not suffer this to interfere with the harmony of the well disposed.

The last leg was the worst of it all. Their bodies were like carcasses. William Nelson is already dying, and they could see that his blind agonies were their future. They caught a seabird, devoured its every part. They caught a fish and did the same. Bligh would tell the story in later years of how his share of the fish was its guts. They have begun to argue over every decision. And there are now thieves among them taking more than their share. Bligh sits over his cutlass in the stern and dreams of how he will punish these mutineers of his smallest command.

They reach the eastern shores of Timor, and not knowing where Kupang and the Dutch settlement lay, move slowly, now against the wind, around to its western shores.

By now Bligh is into the last pages of his pocketbook. He knows he is almost there and his entries become discursive and relaxed. Protocols occupy his mind. He doesn't know how he will be received by the Dutch authorities, or even if he will be believed. His papers, the props of his authority, now become important. He doesn't let them stagger into Kupang. He holds off for one night so that they can come ashore with propriety. In the calm of the bay, he writes, they took *three hours of the most happy and sweetest sleep the men ever had.*

The very last page of the pocketbook has his sketches of the Great Union flag of England and Scotland he has the men sew.

I do all my sailing in libraries and archives. Often with a small sketch of the sails and rigging and their names beside me! The pains and tribulations of my voyaging to read my many one-off pieces of paper are principally jet lag. I often wonder whether I would have the courage or skill to do what the writers of these pages did. I wonder, even more, whether I could be a writer in these circumstances. One doesn't have to like Bligh to treasure the image of him huddled in the stern of the launch, taking every opportunity to put pen and ink to paper, passionately recording whatever he thinks will be useful for sailors coming after him, squeezing his daily navigational calculations around his entries.

I owe Bligh much. For many years I taught my students how to write history out of this pocketbook and these journals. I owe him understanding. I owe him justice. But more than anything I owe him the realism of a crafted story, a crafted true story. I can't think where else that I can begin to pay my dues other than out of the pages he himself has written – and, of course, out of the pages written by those who have been affected by Bligh more closely than I.

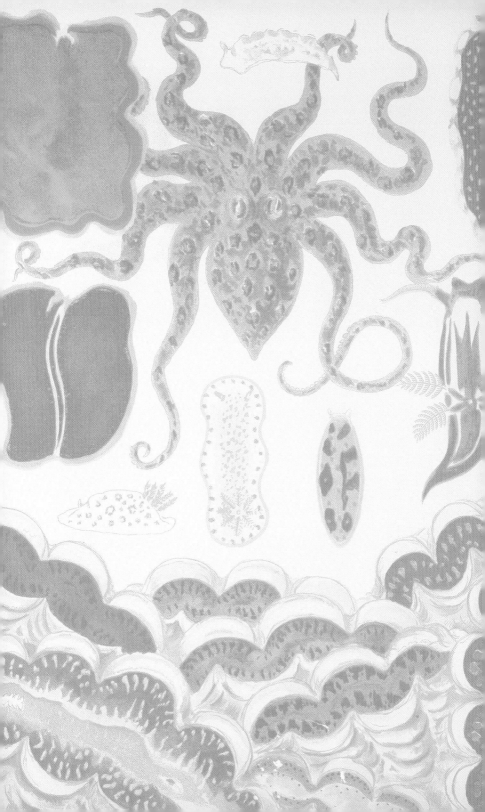

libby gleeson

A LADY LONG RESIDENT IN NEW SOUTH WALES: AN ENCOUNTER

*T*HE PAST IS ANOTHER *country; they do things differently there.* Australian writers, Ethel Turner, Mary Grant Bruce, Nan Chauncy were my childhood reading. All of them are now dead. I remember them as creators of strong narratives with characters I believed in and wanted to be. None would be mistaken for contemporary children's literature, but the difference is a matter of degree. Reading *Seven Little Australians* or *A Little Bush Maid* or *They Found a Cave* is like journeying to a country only a little different from one's own. The landscape and the language are almost familiar. It's rather like a Sydneysider travelling to Melbourne: some words are foreign, the architecture varies but the core of the culture is recognisably the same.

Because I write for young people, I wanted to find a work and a writer of importance in this area who was not familiar: someone who was not part of my childhood reading and who existed in territory less familiar. I wanted to come to the work fresh, writer to writer, uninfluenced by childhood memory. And so I ventured to the first book written for children in this country: *A Mother's Offering to her Children*, by a Lady Long Resident in New South Wales. Printed in Sydney, in 1841 by the *Gazette*, the book now exists as a facsimile edition published in 1979 by The Jacaranda Press. It is a small, hardback book that fits neatly in the hand. The dust jacket features a portrait of Elizabeth, the young daughter of Conrad Martens, painted by her father. She's sitting, demure, head bowed over a book, reading. Her dress and the soft, background landscape of the portrait, place it in the early Victorian era.

What did I expect? My reading of that period is limited to British and American fiction, not necessarily that written for children. They are strong stories, such as Dickens, that reveal the social conditions in industrial England, or adventure tales of journeying to the South Seas. Perhaps the Lady Long

Resident in New South Wales would reveal something of the world of white settlement, the community changing from penal colony to community of free settlers. I was hoping for a literary antecedent that went beyond my childhood reading.

There is a preface addressed to 'Master Reginald Gipps, son of His Excellency Sir George Gipps, Governor of New South Wales and its Dependencies, and of Lady Gipps'. In self-deprecating terms, the 'little work is dedicated, by permission, and the author hopes the incidents it contains may afford him some little entertainment in the perusal: its principal merit is the truth of the subjects narrated …'. Truth. Is this ironic, a preface to a Swiftian tale of wonder? Is it to be taken at face value, a simple statement of what the writer believes?

Already, I am entering a strange land. The opening page has a heading: story or chapter, I'm not sure – Extraordinary Sounds. Then there is a list of names, reminiscent of a cast list for a play script: Mrs Seville, engaged at her needle, Clara, Emma, Amusing themselves by Drawing, Julius, Lucy. Emma speaks – *How very extraordinary those tremendous noises were Mamma, which we heard at the Coolondal Mountain; while you and my brother were from home.*

Dialogue to open the story. A technique I use myself, often. It draws the reader in, gives voice to character immediately. Is this dialogue the same? Do the Lady Long Resident and I share this approach? I read on. Mrs Saville answers her daughter. Clara asks – *Did you ever hear of any similar occurrence, Mamma?* Still further, Clara again says – *Do you know what description of country it was, Mamma?* and then – *What time of the day did the report occur, Mamma?* Julius asks, – *Did you ever hear such sounds accounted for, Mamma, in any way?*

Each view expressed by the mother, each description of a natural phenomenon, each story told later in the work, comes as a response to a question or a comment by one of the children. It is a catechism, formalised, stylised and apparently common in the early part of the nineteenth century. It is structured more like a work for the stage than a novel or a work of non-fiction and yet there is no dramatic tension.

The four children gather around their mother in the evening. Sometimes they bring their various craft activities, sometimes the atlas. I learn nothing of them beyond the group. The book is not about them, it is for them. They are there to learn and the mother is there to teach. And teaching itself is the giving of information, primarily about natural phenomena: geology, botany, stories of swallows and of beetles. Lengthy and dramatic tales are told of shipwrecks and survival and atrocities in the Torres Strait. There are gory details of decapitation and cannibalism. The tale of Eliza Fraser and the shipwreck of the *Stirling Castle* are related, the first 'literary' telling, and then there are a small number of anecdotes of the life of local Aboriginal people.

The children respond graciously to their mother's words: – *Thank you, dear Mamma, it is a very delightful account.* And the mother is quick to invoke God and a moral lesson as the true meaning of what she has to say – *God can, when he sees fit, extricate us from the greatest of calamities.* And – *Oh! My chil-*

dren! How very, very fatal is this habit of putting off from day to day, what should be done immediately; for we know not the day, nor the hour, when time may cease for us: and we be summoned into eternity.

She repeats the claim in the preface: – *I am not at liberty to invent. All is deemed to be true.* Oh to have such confidence. In the process of my own writing I am hesitant and cautious. I question myself and my text for intention and meaning. I try to imagine every possible reading. I am immediately suspicious of those who pronounce possession of 'truth' and so I suspect this Lady. I cannot separate Mrs Saville, the character, from the Lady Long Resident in NSW. I suspect her calm gentility. She infuriates me the way Marmee in *Little Women* used to infuriate me when I read that work as a child. I want a real mother. I want a normal maternal outburst, I want to see emotion other than calm, respectful conversation. I want something other than the prose as constrained as the contents of a middle-class woman's corset. I want to get inside her head.

But how to do that when I know nothing other than that she is a Lady Long Resident in New South Wales?

When I first read this work I sought out a travel guide and found Maurice Saxby's *A History of Australian Children's Literature, 1841–1941*. He states the belief that the Lady Long Resident was Lady Bremer, wife of the naval Captain commissioned to take possession of Northern Australia. In her introduction to the facsimile edition, Rosemary Wighton is confident that this is not so, as Lady Bremer never visited Australia, but no other candidate is nominated.

In a monograph published in 1980, Marcie Muir presents a case for the Lady to have been Charlotte Barton, born Charlotte Waring, in England in 1797. She came to Australia in 1826 to be governess to the children of Hannibal and Maria Macarthur. On board ship she met James Atkinson, a well respected member of colonial society and they became engaged. They were married in 1827 and settled at Oldbury, a property in the Sutton Forest region of New South Wales. Four children were born and when the youngest was only six weeks old, James Atkinson died 'from inflammation brought on by drinking impure water, on the top of Razorback, when heated'. Two years later Charlotte married again, a friend of her late husband, George Barton, but he shortly became a 'furious maniac' and had to be kept under restraint.

The research that identifies Charlotte Barton is compelling. In an early review of the published book, the author is referred to as Mrs Barton. Charlotte and her four children lived for a long time in the Southern Highlands of NSW, the region most described by Mrs Saville in her stories. Finally Charlotte's daughter, Louisa Atkinson, was the first Australian-born woman novelist and in her memoriam notice, reference is made to her mother who '… distinguished herself by the publication of several useful works for children'.

Charlotte, you fascinate me. How do you fit with Mrs Saville? Behind that calm gentility is a woman who has crossed oceans and weathered storms. The poem written at the end of the *Mother's Offering*, 'Lines Written During A Storm in the Bay of Biscay' tells of the near disastrous experience en route to Australia. You bore four children in an age when dying in childbirth was a regular occurrence. Indeed two of your own daughters were to suffer this fate. You came from a relatively comfortable middle-class life in London to live in the bush at some distance from Sydney in an area populated by numerous Aboriginal tribes. You buried one husband and were forced to commit another. All this while nurturing and educating four little ones.

Yet I see none of this in your writing. Instead there are unreadable accounts of volcanoes and grass trees, copper mines and trochus shells. The only pain shown in your writing is that experienced by others: the black woman Jenny and those who suffer at the hands of islanders, post shipwreck. You keep your distance from them and I sense only the vaguest curiosity.

You are white and middle class and educated and you do not reveal yourself. You hide yourself from your reader. Especially as your reader is a child and must learn from what is not in your work as much as from what is.

Whereas we, post Freud, post Eliot, post sixties, post every experience of the twentieth century, do not shy from personal revelation. Ours is not only a journey to the Burning Mountain, to Port Essington or to the Torres Strait, but also a journey in the mind. We seek significance in experiences, relationships and feelings. Our physical world is safe and we seek drama and tension in our inner lives. Your world, Charlotte, was far more hazardous and threatening, and yet you created a calm and reassuring domesticity that to today's reader is simply unbelievable.

I too am a mother. I have never thought of my work as offerings to my children. I ask them to read my manuscripts and I check with them for certain details. I know they are in the work as I am. Unavoidably. My children are there not as shadows of themselves or devices to construct a way of telling a tale but fictionalised. They are part of my characters, boisterous, cheeky, thoughtful, funny, curious, kind, serious, selfless and selfish. These characters are as fully rounded as I can create them and they are there in stories, picture book fictions, for the very young. They are also in longer tales for older children, tales of the lives of families and individuals, growing in contemporary communities, which are sometimes kind, and sometimes not so.

And Truth? Like many novelists I could say I struggle to write as true as I can, but to claim truth would be to lie. My work is as much a construct of its time as is the *Mother's Offering to her Children*. And part of that construction is the offering of me as the author as part of the package. Marketing drives publishing in the same way it drives so many aspects of economic and political life and the writer, not the work, is often what is offered. Were you to come into our time, Charlotte, the Lady Long Resident in NSW would be packaged and delivered to her readership with an extravagant competition. There would be clues to try to work out who this mystery writer is, a highly visible competition to attract participants and at the end, when someone had discovered her identity, the Lady herself would be delivered up as the prize. Dinner with the Lady for two with a bottle of wine thrown in. The Lady for the day as a guest of your school. She'll read from her work, run a workshop, answer any questions no matter how personal. (Where do your ideas come from? How much money do you earn? How old are you?)

When *A Mother's Offering to her Children* was published in 1841 it was written about in both the *Gazette* and the *Australian*. It was deemed a '… useful Christmas present from friends here to friends in England'. And a '… work that embraces a variety of useful and entertaining matter …'. More recent judgments have varied. One writer sees the work as showing a '… charming feeling of a warm loving family', while another feels that the work is '… didactic, and is a thinly disguised and not very interesting lesson in natural science, geology and anthropology'. My support is with the latter. *A Mother's Offering to her Children* is a slight work that sits in the tradition of instructional texts, already giving way in England to more adventurous tales and fictions of family life. It is noteworthy only because it is the earliest known work for children, not for any significant role it played in setting a direction for subsequent writing to follow.

REFINED

MUTTON BIRD OIL

For the relief of
Consumption, Miner's Complaint,
Bronchitis, Catarrh, Asthma, and all
Chest and Lung Troubles; also for
Wasting and Debility arising from
Disease.

DIRECTIONS. ADULTS. One tablespoonful
three times a day.
CHILDREN. One half to one teaspoonful to
be gradually increased as required.

carmel bird

THE CYCLOPEDIA: A SHORT STRANGE SECRET MISTY SMOKY MYSTERIOUS HISTORY

SOMETIMES PEOPLE ASK ME how growing up in Tasmania has affected my work as a fiction writer. I lived in Tasmania for the first twenty-three years of my life, and from the beginning I was fascinated by the short, strange, secret history of the place. I entertained myself quite a bit by reading the books in our house. I still have some of the books, and so I can refer to them in detail, not having to rely on memory.

Among the large and gloomy books which inspired me

were two volumes called *The Cyclopedia of Tasmania*. This was a curious compendium of facts from the state's past, published in 1900. I loved looking at these books. They consisted of page after page of photographs of people and buildings, as well as text, and they were such imposing volumes, so self-important and arresting. Most of the people in them were men with beards and wide, staring eyes. Very, very occasionally there was a picture of a woman such as Miss Marion Oldham who was the Principal of the Wattle Grove State School, but women were generally not part of the main narrative.

There is Mrs Ferrar, who appears seated beside her husband. Mrs Ferrar 'remembers some exciting scenes in connection with the early days of the colony, when the aborigines were as thick as the proverbial bees, and as troublesome as wild beasts'. I wonder if Mrs Ferrar spoke those words. Once Mrs Ferrar was speared and clubbed, but 'happily with no serious results'. The phrase 'speared and clubbed' is one I have always found particularly arresting. It is so plain, so stark, bluntly violent, so inarguable. This prose is much more lively than is usual in *The Cyclopedia*. 'As thick as the proverbial bees, and as troublesome as wild beasts.'

There is a description of 'one of the handsomest shops in the colonies'. This is quite interesting, because the entry in *The Cyclopedia* begins by describing the shop itself, before explaining what Mr A.P. Miller – Chemist, Druggist, and Distiller – does. The shop is so elegant and ornamented, with its bevelled glass and embossed gold lettering, its she-oak drawers with crystal knobs, its windows decorated with designs of Tasmanian wildflowers and birds. Mr Miller was one of the first people in Tasmania to use the oil of the blue gum tree in the manufacture of creams and soaps and ointments. So *The Cyclopedia* is not without its glimpses of literary felicity. I really liked Mr Miller, a character who came to life among hundreds of characters who didn't.

Mostly the prose is incredibly dull. Its very leaden nature stimulated my imagination, and the titles of institutions were enough to set me thinking. Imagine the Church of England Home of Mercy for Fallen Women. Then, there is an absence of children. In a photograph of a giant tree (Tasmania is famous for giant trees) a small girl in a white pinafore and bonnet sits at the root of the tree, while to the left, almost invisible, there sits a woman in black, wearing a stern hat. Both figures have their hands folded on their lap. To the right a man lounges against the base of the tree, his back to the other figures, his hat rather jaunty, his hand on his hip. He stares into the distance. The woman and child suggest themselves as fairy folk. Behind the tree, which reaches up into the heavens beyond the frame, all is misty, smoky, mysterious. How could I not be affected by all this? I was, of course, deeply affected.

Another notable absence from the pictures and the narrative is that of the Chinese population which was actually considerable. Even as a child I wondered about that. This is a white, generally Protestant, serious, respectable history. Yet as I will explain, it awakened and nourished my interest in the stories of indigenous Tasmanians.

The businessmen who subscribed to the publishing costs

of the books were the principal characters in the narrative of
The Cyclopedia. The authors, generally, are not acknowledged,
so it is often impossible to know who was behind the story,
responsible for the language, at any time.

One particularly fascinating section is at the back of
Volume Two – 'Curious Facts of Old Colonial Days'. It
includes entries headed 'State Morals in the Early Days' and
'Strong Drink in Van Diemen's Land'. Then there are six pages
titled 'The Aborigines of Tasmania'. This part has no photographs. It seems to be a little afterthought. It is followed by a
section called 'Miscellaneous'. The section about the Aborigines begins with the information:

'A special interest attaches to the aboriginal inhabitants of
"the garden island" inasmuch as they have become utterly
extinct; and that too within the memory of many persons who
are still in the prime of life.' There follows a selection of notes
from James Bonwick's work *Daily Life and Origin of the Tasmanians*. The extinction is stated as a fact, uninformed by
pathos, let alone outrage.

Now I was prepared to believe what the book said, that
this race of people had 'completely disappeared off the face of
the earth'. I found the idea remarkable and horrifying, and it is
not only with hindsight that I say I felt there was something
really creepy about the prose itself, this smooth, confident
story of what was being named 'extinction'. 'They have
become utterly extinct.' 'Extinct' was not then a word often,
or ever, used in ordinary conversation. I was interested in it. It
sounded like a whip.

When I was very young I went to the Hobart Museum where I saw the tiny skeleton of Truganini who was supposed to have been the last of the Tasmanian Aborigines. I had never even seen a human skeleton before, let alone the skeleton of the last member of a lost race of people. I felt awe and a dreadful, shocked sadness. I remember the skeleton as being somehow unrelated to human life, so tiny, so museumy – more like the remains of a bandicoot or something. So *this* was extinction.

Then there was another book I used to pore over, a cheap green-bound volume published in 1928, *Tasmania's North-East*. This one is written in a much more lively and personal style, and I really liked that about it. The author, Mr A.W. Loone, invents headings such as 'Child Shockingly Mutilated' and 'Experience With Grasses' and 'The Joke that Failed'. This was clearly a better class of story. The author also quotes James Bonwick, but the burden of his narrative is one of deep compassion and a very real sorrow. He believes the accepted version of the extinction of the race, but his regret is palpable. Other texts I read were informed with a smug congratulation that extinction had been achieved. A most curious feature of this book is that its final chapter, called a 'Conclusion', concerns three important Tasmanian Aborigines. It felt to me even as a child that it was a peculiar way to end a book that seemed to be about the pioneers and adventurers and early settlers of the district. It was not usual to end on this note. It is no afterthought, but rather a lament which insists on being spoken, which sits most powerfully as the final statement of the book.

The last glossy illustration is a reproduction of the Thomas Bock portrait of the Aborigine known as Jack of Cape Grim. One of the three Aborigines in the last chapter is Truganini, one is King Billy, and the third is Mathinna.

The first sentence in this chapter says: 'The history of Mathinna is melancholy in the extreme.'

The entire hidden tragedy and mystery, lit with the flashes of what horrors I knew of the fate of Tasmanian Aborigines, exercised a fascination over my early imagination, but possibly my heart was most deeply touched by the story of this girl. Mathinna. This little girl. There was a smudgy black and white reproduction of Thomas Bock's portrait of her in some other book belonging to my father, but I no longer have that book. I used to stare and stare at the picture, convinced somehow that the sitter was looking into my soul. Or I was looking into hers. (A portrait of the Princes in the Tower actually had a similar effect on me. I would keep returning to these sweet boys – they resembled girls – who had been murdered and disposed of, never to be found.) I can't recall when I first saw the picture of Mathinna in colour, but I had imagined that her dress was pink. In fact it is red. The redness seems now to be somehow very significant. I recall my mother telling me that it was actually right to put red shoes on little girls, but wrong to put red shoes on little boys. In fact I really expected Mathinna should have been wearing a white dress. I would have given her a white dress, I thought. Did somebody agonise over the colour? Or was it just that there was a handy piece of red cloth? I was very attracted to portraits of children, and I had several prints of these framed on my bedroom wall, and I thought about them a lot. I am quite sentimental – I have to tell you that for me this picture of Mathinna is the saddest, sweetest, dearest image, and its meaning for me is entwined with my own early life and early reading, as a child, in Tasmania.

Let me tell you what I know about the story of Mathinna.

In 1833, two years before Mathinna was born, her people of the South West tribe were captured by George Augustus Robinson as part of his re-location program, and removed to the Aboriginal settlement on Flinders Island. This settlement was part of a failed experiment in the management of the native people of Van Diemen's Land. Mathinna was born on Flinders Island and was separated from her family, sent to live with the schoolteacher as part of a policy to educate the children in white ways as early as possible in their lives. She was in fact the second child her parents had lost to the white authorities. So from the very beginning of her life Mathinna was alienated from her own people. Her name was to begin with 'Mary' but was later changed by white folk to 'Mathinna', suggesting to me a rather complex and bewildering confusion of black and white identity.

The Governor of the colony in Van Diemen's Land was John Franklin, and in 1838 he and his wife Jane visited the Aboriginal settlement at Wybalenna on Flinders Island. They inspected the place and were entertained by the Aborigines with song and dance, and they gave out gifts of beads, handkerchiefs, knives, and marbles. Two years later the Governor and his Lady returned to Wybalenna, and this time they arranged for the child Mary (soon to become known as Mathinna) who was now five, to live with them at Government House in Hobart Town.

Mathinna was suddenly elevated to the status of a child of colonial aristocracy. She shared a governess with Eleanor, the daughter of John Franklin, and rode in the carriage with Lady Franklin. It was at this time that Lady Franklin commissioned Thomas Bock to paint Mathinna's portrait. Eleanor Franklin kept a diary in which she mentioned Mathinna only twice, a fact that I see as significant in what it reveals about Eleanor's relationship or lack of it with Mathinna. I will quote these entries which I first read when I was about twelve.

Eleanor wrote: 'The last Aborigines were caught about a fortnight ago, and sent to Flinders Island, so that our little native girl is the only one remaining here. She is improving I think, though it will be a long time before she becomes quite civilised.'

The other entry, in which Eleanor copies out a letter written by Mathinna, is, in the context of Mathinna's life, one of the most moving and touching passages I have ever read in its simplicity and its vivid revelation of a life. It is a statement in the form of a letter to Mathinna's stepfather (her own father died when she was two). It seems to me that there is a conflation of three fathers – the stepfather, Governor Franklin, and God. The letter is dated 14 November 1841, and it reads:

'Mathinna is six years old. Her mother Eveline, father, modern name Hannibal, Cape Sorell tribe. I am good little girl. I have pen and ink cause I am good little girl. I do love my father. I have got a doll and shift and a petticoat. I read. My father I thank thee for sleep. I have got red frock. Like my father. Come here to see my father. I have got sore feet and shoes and stockings and I am very glad. All great ships. Tell my father two rooms.'

This period in Mathinna's life, when she had her own bedroom and her pet possum, when she danced for visitors in her English clothes, did not last long. Two years in fact. Two years during which time she became the pet of the Europeans, but could no longer relate to her own people. The Franklins left Van Diemen's Land and returned to England in 1843, leaving her behind. She was placed in the Queen's Orphan School in Hobart where she was utterly different from and unacceptable to the other children. A year later she was back on Flinders Island living with the schoolmaster. Fanny Cochrane, an Aboriginal girl who was Mathinna's age, and who in fact lived to be seventy, was living there as well. The Aborigines at Wybalenna were dying. Mathinna's stepfather died when Mathinna was eleven – her mother was already dead. When she was twelve Mathinna was returned to the Queen's Orphan School.

At New Norfolk, north-west of Hobart, the Governor had a country house which Mathinna had visited when she was a member of the Franklin household. She was now taken there for a Christmas treat, as an orphan from the school. Governor and Lady Denison gave a big party, with plum pudding and gifts. There was a tent on the lawn for white folk and a tent for black folk. The Europeans were very interested in the Aborigines, since such people had not been seen in public in southern Van Diemen's Land for a long time. There was a genuine desire to give the Aborigines a good time at the party, but there was also a sense in which they were a collection of freaks on show. It is so sad and poignant to imagine Mathinna as one of the Aborigines who played and danced for the European audience, she who not long before would have been among the privileged white children herself. And it was only a day outing. In the evening the carriages took the visitors back to the Orphan School.

The Orphan School was an abject Dickensian place of overcrowding, disease, hunger and punishment. The Denisons were interested in trying to improve the conditions, paying visits and taking gifts, and giving prizes for good work. By the time Mathinna left the school at the age of sixteen, she was the only Aboriginal left. She went to live at the tragic settlement at Oyster Cove where the dwindling group of Aborigines were dying of loneliness, disease and broken hearts.

By the time she was twenty-one Mathinna was trading her body for alcohol, and one night when she was drunk she fell into the water, and she drowned.

I try to match the end of this story with the image of the child in the red dress, and I fancy that in the soft hands, gentle smile, and in the intense and searching eyes of the portrait, I can feel the tragedy of the child's future already written.

You can see that I have a special affection for and re-lationship with this portrait. I have carried a framed print of it round with me for a long time. Some years ago I went to live in an old house in Melbourne. I was using one of the rooms as a storeroom for the time being. But for some reason I banged a nail in the wall and put up one picture, the picture of Math-inna. In the middle of the night, the ceiling of that room came crashing down. Now I realise that that ceiling was ancient and unstable, and that I had disturbed it by hammering the nail into the wall, but I choose to wonder. Would the ceiling have descended if the picture had been of my father in his cricket team?

When I was discussing this essay with Marion, the editor of the book, I told her the anecdote of the ceiling. That night, another piece of ceiling, this time in the bedroom, fell down, disturbed, I like to think, by my telling of the story. I have now had all the ceilings in the house replaced. They are superb. Growing up in Tasmania has affected my reading, my writing, and my ceilings.

lucy frost

DISPLAYING TRUGERNANNA

IN 1947 WHEN I was six years old, the skeleton of Trugernanna was taken off display in the Tasmanian Museum and Art Gallery in Hobart. That same year, in the late August heat of north Texas, I began school and started reading about a couple of twerps named Dick and Jane whose saccharine existence was enlivened by a dog named Spot. Infinitely more dramatic and complicated narratives spiced my own day and night dreams. Some of the stories I shared with my sister Ruth, especially when we went on excursions to our favourite picnic place, the upside-down mountain of Palo Dura Canyon. On our drive south from Amarillo across the almost featureless landscape of the high plains, we always stopped at a little museum in a small town called Canyon. All I remember of the museum is a diorama with miniature Indians on horseback streaking across the plains from which living Indians had been driven decades before. We didn't know that, of course. Our Apache warriors existed not in historical time, but in the fantasy time of children's heads. Each warrior, dazzling in his headdress of eagle feathers, controlled a horse with one hand while holding aloft a tomahawk with the other. Ruth and I pressed our faces against the glass of the diorama, as if somehow this would bring us closer to the fascinating figures. Shut up again in the back seat of our father's unreliable post-war Studebaker, we would tell ourselves into the world of the diorama, becoming wild Indians on wild horses. The tedium of driving down straight highways no longer mattered.

If in 1947 I had been a child in Hobart, instead of Amarillo, I'm sure I would have pressed my nose against the glass of the museum's diorama where a life-size Trugernanna kneels before the fire, dressed only in a string of seashells. And then I could have stared into the display case featuring the articulated skeleton identified by a sign: 'Lallah Rooke, or Truganini, the last Tasmanian Aboriginal'. The museum offered Trugernanna both 'denuded of flesh' (as her skeleton was described in a contemporary account), and re-fleshed in plaster of Paris.

Although I have never returned to Texas since I left in 1953 and cannot be sure what has happened to the diorama of Apache warriors, I would be very surprised if they remained to lure white children like me into the fantasy of a vanished other. In Hobart, however, Trugernanna continues to kneel before the fire, watched by her husband Woorrady and a boy of six or seven, the child she in reality could never bear after sealers had infected her with a 'loathesome disease', probably gonorrhoea. Father and son wait patiently for mum to cook an enormous crayfish and serve it to her nuclear family. This is a story of Trugernanna, but it is not her story.

A few weeks ago I stood in the room housing the Aboriginal collection, and watched as children passed through on their way to this summer's most popular exhibit, 'Dinosaurs of Darkness', attracting some 15,000 visitors according to the Hobart *Mercury*. The diorama takes up one entire wall of the room housing the Aboriginal collection, and nothing else can begin to compete with it for dramatic effect. Naturally the children on their way to see the dinosaurs noticed the naked black boy reaching out to touch the shoulder of his kneeling mother, and they detoured over to get as close to the glass as a railing allows. Who are these people? the children wanted to know. Their parents floundered around for answers, trying to historicise the fantasy before them. At Woorrady's feet lies the only stab at interpretation, a sign entitled 'social organisation'. 'There were three levels of social organisation,' it begins, droning on through a taxonomic account of the hearth group, band, tribe, until (if you make it through to the end), a politically charged word breaches the bland surface: 'Prior to European invasion, the population has been estimated at 3,000–4,000 people'. 'Invasion', not settlement, and yet in its context evasive. What is happening here, to this family before my eyes? What is the story of the people I am looking at? The

sign provides today's children with no more honest an interpretation of violent colonial contact in Tasmania than the
display of Indians and tomahawks told me in 1947 about
the violent history of north Texas. At the Tasmanian Museum
and Art Gallery, non-indigenous children are still taught the
colonising gaze.

How I wish that their experience were different, that one
day as they pressed against the railing Trugernanna would rise
from her demurely kneeling position, turn towards them, walk
through the glass veil, and begin talking. 'She was partial to
conversation', wrote a journalist in the Hobart *Mercury* the
day after her death on 8 May 1876, and 'always willing to give
such information as was within her knowledge'. Trugernanna
was born about 1812, less than a decade after the first autho-
rised settlement in Van Diemen's Land. Her stories would
have spanned the entire period of settlement and reached back
to the earlier years when sealers and whalers began disrupting
Aboriginal communities. To the *Mercury*'s journalist, the old
woman was primarily a curiosity who had moved with the
Dandridge family from Oyster Cove to a house just four
blocks down Macquarie Street from the museum awaiting her:
'Her short, stout figure, red turban, and dusky features were
known far and wide, and always attracted great attention'.

There were some who understood her importance as a
witness to history. James Erskine Calder talked with Trugernanna when he was writing the book he would call *Some
Account of the Wars, Extirpation, Habits, etc of the Native Tribes
of Tasmania* (1875). He asked her why she went with James

Augustus Robinson on his 'Friendly Mission' to bring in those yet alive after the Black War. 'Mr. Robinson,' she told Calder, 'was a good man and could speak our language, and I said I would go with him and help him.' It was 'the best thing to do … I hoped we would save all my people that were left'. From the first of Robinson's expeditions Trugernanna served as 'one of the "ambassadors" who went forward to meet the local mob, telling them "why we have come and that our people were all being killed and it was no use fighting any more, and Mr Robinson was our friend, and would take us all to a good place".' She was, says Henry Reynolds, a patriot with 'a serious political agenda'. But in the diorama, the wife and mother sitting passively before the fire bears no resemblance to an ambassador or to one of the guides who helped Robinson through a landscape as foreign to them as to the white man, terrain never previously walked by a European, too rugged ever to be tamed into farms and towns, and now designated a wilderness area preserved as world heritage. Trugernanna might have been remembered as an intrepid explorer who went with the white man on a remarkable, and successful, venture of exploration. But she wasn't. And isn't.

Members of the Royal Society saw to that. For them, Trugernanna was a collectible. The day after her death announced, Dr James Agnew wrote to the Colonial Secretary asking that Trugernanna's body be given over to the Royal Society for its museum. His argument emphasised her value as a tourist drawcard:

At times like the present when the study of races occupies so much learned attention, types of this kind are of high value and it may safely be affirmed that in future years no specimen in our national museum would possess greater interest for the learned & scientific traveller from other lands.

Trugernanna had become valuable because hers was the last name on a countdown to extinction.

The prelude to countdown began with the Friendly Mission during which Robinson, helped by Trugernanna and the others, persuaded Aborigines from all parts of the island to end their conflict with the colonists and come in to the settled areas. In 1833 the people 'brought in' agreed to go temporarily to Flinders Island in Bass Strait, on the understanding that they would later return to the mainland. There, at a settlement called Wybalenna, two hundred survivors of the Black War discovered that the promises made by Robinson would not be kept. They were marooned in a place which was for them unhealthy, as it was not for the convicts who lived and worked there. Respiratory illnesses struck the Aborigines again and again, and they died from pneumonia, tuberculosis, influenza. In 1847, after fourteen years of exile, the forty-six who yet lived, including a few children born at Wybalenna, were once more put on a ship and transported over the sea. Their new home was to be at Oyster Cove, forty kilometres south of Hobart, sufficiently removed from town to placate those burghers frightened by the mere idea of 'a native'. Oyster

Cove had the added advantage of costing little. A gang of convicts had been sent there a few years before to construct a female prison on the site, but that project had been abandoned when it was decided to use instead a prison hulk moored closer to town, and presumably more convenient for settlers who wanted to hire convict women (as they did not plan to hire Aboriginal women).

The Aborigines who returned were initially an undifferentiated group as far as the general public was concerned. Those colonists and travellers who went down to Oyster Cove and signed the visitors' book could scarcely be expected to remember by name everyone they met, and in the early years of return, the Aborigines in residence kept changing anyway. Men came and went on whaling voyages, children came and went from the Queen's Orphan School, and anyone might be off hunting or visiting. As the numbers decreased with yearly deaths and no new births, there were fewer names to remember. Conveniently for those who might have found difficulty with Aboriginal languages, most tribal names had been changed. Trugernanna appeared in government records as 'Lallah Rookh', named by Robinson for an 'Oriental' princess from a narrative poem popular in England before the barely educated bricklayer sailed off to make a name for himself in Van Diemen's Land. At least we have a tribal name for the woman who became Lallah Rookh, even though its spelling and pronunciation remain debatable. Once, shortly before she died, a man invited her to dinner, determined to resolve the matter. Over and over he asked her to repeat the name: 'I

importuned her so much about the proper pronunciation …
that she at last grew impatient, rolled and flashed her eye, and
called me, right out, a fool'.

No tribal name survives for William Lanne, or Lanni or
Lanny or Lanney, sometimes called simply 'Billy' in the government records, known to the whalers with whom he sailed
as 'King Billy'. Lanne was about seven years old when his
family, one of the last 'brought in', left their tribal lands on the
west coast for the settlement on Flinders Island, and when
the exiles returned to live at Oyster Cove, he was sent initially
to the Queen's Orphan School. On 3 March 1869, a few
weeks after returning from a whaling voyage on the *Runnymede*, Lanne died in his room at 'The Dog and Partridge',
Barrack Street, Hobart, aged about thirty-three. As the last
male name on the dwindling list of returned exiles at Oyster
Cove, Lanne attracted the attention of collectors for rival
museums. On one side was Dr William Crowther, who wanted
the kudos he could see coming his way if he managed to ship
Lanne's skeleton to the museum of Britain's Royal College of
Surgeons. According to Crowther, only a fool could 'suppose
that a paltry little place like Tasmania had a better right' to this
unique artefact than London.

The gentlemen of the Royal Society of Tasmania thought
otherwise. Arguing their case for the local museum, they
insisted that their claim to 'possession of the skeleton of the
last male aboriginal of the Colony is altogether paramount to
that of any other scientific institution in the world'.

To this Museum reference will naturally be made in future years for all details of information respecting a race which will then have ceased to exist. Although it already possesses the skeleton of a female it is evident that a male skeleton is required to complete the series, and we would beg respectfully to point out the discredit that would attach to any Government, if, under similar circumstances, they permitted so essential an element of a national collection to be lost to the country. The Council freely admit the claims which science in general has upon these valuable relics, and it is therefore their intention to have them carefully photographed on a large scale in order that copies may be presented not only to the Museum of the Royal College of Surgeons, but to any other kindred institutions by which they are likely to be appreciated. The Council will also afford all facilities within their power, for the execution of casts of such portions of the skeleton as may be specially interesting.

Unbeknownst to Dr Agnew when he wrote this letter on behalf of the Royal Society, his fellow medico William Crowther had already cut off Lanne's head.

Crowther emerges as arrogant, manipulative, totally self-centred, and a bully determined to get what he wanted. First, he got a coroner's order to move Lanne's body from the room where he died to the deadhouse at the General Hospital where Crowther was honorary medical officer. He then told the newly appointed and far junior house surgeon, George Stokell, that 'the body was his, that the Col. Sec^y had given it to him & he said he would have it'. Stokell, however, had already received unequivocal instructions from the rightly suspicious Colonial Secretary 'not to allow any mutilation of the body of the Aboriginal Native "Billy" now lying dead in the Hospital', and despite the pressure, he stood up to the overbearing Crowther: 'I told him that the Col. Sec^y had instructed me that no one should touch or mutilate the body'. Crowther switched to flattery, and Stokell succumbed. Yes, he would be delighted to visit Crowther at home. Most probably the doctor was a bully in that arena as well. Certainly the mutilation of Lanne's corpse became a Crowther family affair – father led the charge, a son enrolled at the General Hospital as pupil to his father helped out, and Mrs Crowther acted as decoy to distract Dr Stokell, whose self-confessed naiveté is quite overwhelming.

> He asked me to go to his house at 6PM. I said I could not go at that hour but I promised to be there at 8 P.M. I started for Dr C's at 7.30, I reached Dr C's & C was not there – Mrs C. kept me there talking. That he would not be long before he was home.
>
> I got back to Hospital about 9. I asked man (Knights) at the gate if Dr. C had been there. He said Dr C & his son had been there & gone. I went straight in dead House – I found the door locked – I opened it. I looked into the coffin – & saw that the skull of Lanne

had been removed & another skull had been substituted, the substituted skull had come from the dissecting Room.

Stokell was in deep trouble. Desperate, he curried favour with Crowther's rivals, cutting off Lanne's hands and feet, and giving them to the Royal Society. Crowther's collectible was spoiled. If the locals could not have Lanne's skeleton intact for their museum, they would at least deprive Londoners of the trophy. 'The last Tasmanian male' could hardly go on display with such obvious bits missing.

On 6 March a funeral was held for Lanne, organised and paid for by the captain of the *Runnymede*, who acted as pall-bearer, along with 'three coloured seamen, John Bull, a native of the Sandwich Islands, Henry Whalley, a half-caste native of Kangaroo Island, South Australia, and Alexander Davidson, an American'. Despite a valiant effort by the whaling community to bestow upon the ceremony some of the decorum for which they were rarely known, rumours were rife, as three gentlemen of Hobart informed the Colonial Secretary: 'It is openly stated & generally believed that the body buried today in St David's Churchyard as that of William Lanni has been shamefully mutilated before interment'. Well into the twentieth century, a Crowther descendant would remember and repeat a ditty learned in childhood:

King Billy's dead. Crowther has his head
Stokell has his hands and feet.
My feet, my feet, my poor black feet
That used to be so gritty
They're not on board the *Runnymede*
They're somewhere in this city.

Trugernanna worried. The 'last Tasmanian Aborigine', people began to call her. But she wasn't. She wasn't even the last survivor from the Friendly Mission. At the settlement on Flinders Island, a daughter was born to two of those 'brought in', Tanganutura and Nicermenic. This baby, who entered the official records as Fanny Cochrane, was among the remnant returned to Van Diemen's Land. In 1857 she escaped the dwindling lists of Oyster Cove when she married William Smith and moved with him to a farm where their family grew to eleven children. Other Aboriginal women had never been on the government records. They were gone from Van Deiemen's Land before the Black War, taken by sealers to islands throughout the Bass Strait, and as far away as Kangaroo Island. Perhaps one was the mother of William Lanne's pall-bearer, the so-called 'half-caste' Henry Whalley.

These others could not protect Trugernanna from the consequences of her fate as colonial symbol. On 8 May 1876 Mrs Dandridge reported to the government officials: 'It is with deep regret I have to report the death of "Lallah Rookh" the last Tasmanian Aborigine'. Three days later, an unnamed correspondent reminded readers of the *Mercury* of how anxious

Trugernanna had been about what would happen to her body: 'Just before the true heiress of the inheritance we have usurped, passed away, she said to Mrs Dandridge, her benefactress, and to a gentleman or two present, "Don't let them cut me, but bury me behind one of the mountains".' If many, and perhaps most, Tasmanians wanted Trugernanna buried rather than denuded of flesh and put on display in the museum, the contingent did not include members of the Royal Society, whose eager letter sent to the Colonial Secretary I have already quoted. No, said the Colonial Secretary in reply, and on 10 May sent out a press release to the editors of the *Mercury* and *Tribune*:

> The Government have received an application from the Council of the Royal Society for the body of Trucanini (Lallah Rookh) the last representative of the aboriginal race of Tasmania ... This application has been refused, and the Government have given orders for the decent interment of the corpse, but to prevent a recurrence of the unseemly scenes which were enacted in March 1869, it has been deemed expedient to inter the body at the Cascades in a vacant spot immediately in front of the Chapel – The funeral will take place at noon tomorrow, and will be conducted at the expense of the Government by Mr William Hamilton the well known undertaker. – The service will be performed by the Rev[d] Canon Parsons, and any friends and sympathizers are invited to attend.

But the funeral did not take place at noon, the undertaker was bypassed, and few friends or sympathisers were invited. Shortly before midnight, a posse of armed men rode with a cart carrying Trugernanna's body through deserted Hobart streets, and up towards Mount Wellington, where since 1828 women had been incarcerated in the Female House of Correction, known during convict days as the female factory at Cascades. A select group, including a reporter from the *Mercury*, gathered within the high walls of the stark convict space, and stood watching.

> Previous to the lid being screwed down several spectators, our reporter among the rest, were shown the face of the deceased Queen, and one lady, of eccentric habits, and who assumes to herself a title as high as that of poor Trucanini, touched the face, as if to make 'assurance doubly sure'. All this time the bell in the reformatory yard was tolling, and as none of the inmates of the institution, a few of the officials and servants excepted, were to be seen in the spacious enclosure, a death-like silence pervaded the place. The coffin screwed down, the spectators assembled in the chapel. They did not number, including some children, more than twenty-five.
> … We understand that a monument of some kind is to be erected over the grave, and Mr Graves has been requested to write an epitaph for it. He has willingly undertaken the task, and proposes that it shall be inscribed in both the English and native languages.

Many people who had intended to pay their respects to the cortége felt cheated by this subterfuge. Readers of the *Mercury*, however, were reminded of the precedent to be avoided:

> The requirements of so-called science, which in our case judging by what took place in March, 1869, means the indecorous selfishness of some member of the medical profession to secure to himself what his brethren desired on the part of all, and the determination of the profession to out-wit a brother medico, or some paid – in honour or cash – agent of a foreign society, imposed on Government the cruel necessity of giving to the last of the aborigines of this Island what bears so near an approach to a felon's grave that the necessity infers a disgrace on us all. ... It is a humiliating reflection, and we envy not the feelings of the unknown gentleman whose zeal in behalf of his so-called science, and whose desire to receive the thanks of some learned Society, are credited with having imposed on the Government of the Colony the necessity of taking so unexceptional a means of preserving the body from the sacrilegious hands that would, probably, had the means been allowed him, made merchandise of the body yesterday laid in the court yard of the Cascades establishment.

Since the *Mercury* had covered extensively the enquiry Crowther faced after Lanne's death, it seems rather coy to refer to an 'unknown gentleman' in this bombastic editorial.

The medico himself, for whatever reason, apparently shied away from the body of Trugernanna.

The Royal Society, however, was still in there fighting. Two months after the burial, Agnew sent another letter. Since 'all due rites of burial have now been publically accorded to deceased', it is 'difficult to conceive that any portion of an enlightened & rational community could object to have the skeleton carefully preserved in our National Collection'. No, came the reply though more muted and accompanied by no press release – the government considered 'it would be premature to exhume the body'. And then, third time lucky. In December 1878, Agnew won. His request 'to secure the skeleton of the Aborigine, Truganini, who was buried at the Cascade Establishment in May 1876', had been granted 'on the understanding that the skeleton shall not be exposed to public view but be decently deposited in a secure resting place where it may be accessible by special permission to scientific men for scientific purposes'. The removal was no secret. On 14 December 1878, *The Weekly Examiner* reported that 'the body of Truganini, the last of the Tasmanian aboriginals, which was buried in the graveyard attached to the Cascades Factory, has been exhumed, the bones denuded of the flesh, and the skeleton handed over to the Royal Society for scientific purposes. Our contemporary states that owing to the peculiar nature of the soil of the Cascades Burial Ground, the body when exposed was found to be in a wonderful state of preservation.' More than thirty years later, in 1912, an old man named Fred Seager told the photographer J.W. Beattie, 'that he was the only one alive now that knew about the "King Billy" & "Trucanini" "business", and gave me a few particulars'. Seager, who as superintendent of the Colonial Hospital had presented eye-witness testimony at the public enquiry into the dismemberment of Lanne, said that he had been present when the body of Trugernanna was dug up:

> … they got a couple of convicts, who were under sentence for murder, to open the grave & get the coffin out.
>
> The vault was full of water, and when they opened the coffin the water poured out of it, and the body seemed to be pulpy, the flesh was just like *mutton fat*, Seager said, 'You just sludged it off the bones as if it were fat!' All the 'fat' was put back in the Coffin again, [the coffin] closed up, & consigned to the vault, the whole being arranged as if nothing had occurred. Seager thought that this peculiar state of the body was due to mineralised water.

The spectre of Trugernanna's flesh, reburied boneless in the coffin, haunts me …

Flesh in a coffin, bones in a box. The box tagged with a curatorial number, and labelled. And kept within Hobart's grand new museum building. But where were the learned travellers from far-off lands, those latter-day Magi following the star of science? Their absence did not matter: in all correspondence from the Royal Society requesting the bodies first of Lanne and then Trugernanna, the paramount argument was the importance of collecting for a 'national' museum. Scientific knowledge was consistently written into second place. The depths of passion aroused by collecting may bewilder many of us, and yet we know that works of art too famous ever to be displayed are stolen from art galleries around the world to feed the fanaticism of collectors. The collectors of the Royal Society had Trugernanna's skeleton in their museum, and that was what they wanted. They were the reason for separating the bones from her flesh, but this does not explain how and why the bones moved from their box to become a display.

It has been said that in the 1890s, the museum's 'curator, Alexander Morton, was about to throw [a] battered old fruit box on to the rubbish heap when he "just happened to catch the writing – very indistinct – of the tag label, and the skeleton was saved" '. In this apocryphal version, the museum is an institution where happenstance rules. The actions taken seem considerably more deliberate. The bones were sent to Melbourne to be articulated into a skeleton under the professional eye of Australia's leading anthropologist, Baldwin Spencer. The Tasmanian Museum and Art Gallery then violated the original terms of acquisition by putting the articulated skeleton on public display. Ian Anderson, descendant of Tasmanian Aborigines, reads the display of Trugernanna's skeleton for the forty years from 1904 to 1947 as 'a totem of triumphant colonialism. The displayed skeleton, and the historical figure of TRUGGERNANNA has been embellished with a potent discourse of extinction. As a colonial symbol TRUG-ER-NAN-NE signifies the land empty of natives, and declares the colonial period over.' The brave and intelligent young woman who went with Robinson in the hope of saving the remnant of her defeated clansmen was employed to say 'full-stop'.

In pondering the deep and traumatising wrongs done to Trugernanna and to the Palawa people whose homeland is the island which has become my home, I have been thinking about the connection between the museum display and the creation of 'Australia'. The display was in a literal sense of the term, post-colonial. Designed in the early days of Federation, its symbolic politics reached out to the project of constructing nation. The needs of nation were different from those of the colonial society which had both eulogised and dishonoured the body of Trugernanna in 1876. Already 'Van Diemen's Land' had been wiped from the map as the somewhere-else of convicts. 'Tasmania' would in the future attract free emigrants, and generate narratives appropriate to a civil society. Sometimes, however, re-packaged history is more easily articulated than absorbed, and the *Mercury* was still trying to push away the convicts when Trugernanna died. In a history lesson for its readers, the newspaper used 'the last' to draw yet another line between the present and an admittedly violent, indeed barbaric, past:

In 1816 the number of aborigines then in the island was roughly estimated at seven thousand … It may almost be said that with the advent of the English began the war of extermination. Some awful deeds were done in this island during the early days of its colonisation. Being a penal settlement, all the sweepings of the English gaols were at that time transported hither – wicked, desperate, bloodthirsty men, caring little for their own lives and less for the lives of others. From these hardened criminals the blacks suffered severely ... As for the aged lady whose death we to-day record, her disappearance from the scene is rendered additionally interesting and important from the fact that with her, for the first time in human annals, dies out the last of a race, a race which doubtless has had its home in this island from time immemorial, and which never knew the meaning of suffering, wretchedness, and contempt until the English, with their soldiers, bibles, and rum-puncheons, came and dispossessed them of their heritage.

The Aborigines have gone, and their destroyers were another people, not us. Sometimes it seems as if the record were stuck in its groove, the same sentiments heard over and over, into the twenty-first century when a Prime Minister can latch onto the notion of black armband history, and say it belongs to someone else, not to him. The problem remains, how do we tell a story of ourselves which actually fits the evidence?

Though the problem persists, the stakes change. A quarter of a century after the *Mercury* described the local experience of colonial contact as a 'war of extermination', men framed a Constitution in which the Aboriginal peoples of the newly federated states were not to be counted in the census, on the assumption that they were members of a vanishing race.

The 'doomed race theory' was fostered by imperialist readings of evolutionary science. By the 1930s, the theory had fallen into disrepute within the scientific community, and demoted to the status of myth. In Hobart's prestigious museum, however, the display underpinned by the discredited ideology continued to perpetrate the myth which blinded the populace to the Aboriginal people in their midst. No hint of even a possibility of continuing and unbroken Tasmanian Aboriginal culture, protocols, and practices was evident in the display case which featured the articulated skeleton surrounded by artefacts coding the Palawa as extinct *because* they were primitive – see their spears and baskets and stone implements and necklaces made from shells. According to the inexorable laws of science, ran the logic, they *must* give way to 'higher forms' (the English) and disappear. Nothing to do with history, nothing to do with those English 'soldiers, bibles, and rum-puncheons, [who] came and dispossessed them of their heritage'. No mention of that 'war of extermination'. Until after the Second World War, the Tasmanian Museum and Art Gallery continued to display the remains of Trugernanna on behalf of the nation's future, holding out a promise that what had happened in the island state would happen as well on the island continent.

While the curator responsible for selecting, placing, and labelling items in the exhibit may not have pondered its function in imagining 'nation', all museum displays require interpretation within the discourses available at the time. Museums, as Stephen Dubin has said, 'are important venues in which a society can define itself and present itself publicly.

Museums *solidify* culture, endow it with a tangibility, in a way few other things do.' Adults remember the museums they visited as children, as I do the little museum in north Texas. Images from the displays stick in the mind. We may remember the images, and yet be quite oblivious to the struggles for interpretation surrounding them. In the case of Trugernanna's skeleton, we can retrieve the museum's interpretation because a photograph was taken by J.W. Beattie, the same man who would later record Fred Seager's account of digging up the coffin buried at the female factory. Beattie's photograph was published in *The Tasmanian Mail* of 24 June 1905 under the heading, 'An Absolutely Unique Exhibit: Tasmanian Museum and Art Gallery – The Last of a Race'. Today that photograph travels the ether because a woman of Native American descent wrote a poem about Trucanini; the poem was selected for an anthology of modern American poetry published by Oxford University Press in 2000; a website has been designed as a multimedia companion to the printed anthology; and within the website is 'A Gallery of Trucanini' where you can follow Trugernanna's fate as visual representation.

Most of the representations on the website are photographs, the first taken at Oyster Cove on a March day in 1858. The local Anglican Bishop, Francis Russell Nixon, came down by boat from Hobart Town and unloaded the expensive and cumbersome equipment he had imported as soon as the wet-plate system made it possible for an amateur to squint behind the camera. Fascinated by the process of mechanical reproduction, Nixon had mastered the techniques of quickly coating, sensitising, exposing and developing the negative plates. He must have set up a darkroom tent close to the huts where he posed Trugernanna and the others. Grim faces stare into the camera, resigned to repeating yet again the experience of captivity, of being 'taken'. From the plates of Nixon and his fellow recorders of the countdown to death at Oyster Cove, thousands of images have been generated. For years before Trugernanna's death, her photographs had been advertised in the local newspapers as just the sort of souvenir to send Home to your friends and relations. Later, the images were re-deployed for postcards. How bitter the irony that a body rendered sterile after contact with the invaders should be reproduced with such endless mechanical fecundity.

Trugernanna had experienced image-taking before Nixon unloaded his stereoscopic camera at Oyster Cove, though never on a mass scale and not since before the exile to Flinders Island. It was within the heroic mode that those who went with Robinson on the Friendly Mission had originally been represented. Robinson, with an eye to history, ensured that the Mission was commemorated. His Aboriginal companions had been sketched, painted, and sculpted by artists who could and did replicate and sell the images to those who valued 'art'. Though most of the representations were portraits, Benjamin Duterrau's group study, *The Conciliation* (1840), is recognised as 'the first history painting attempted in Australia'. In the composition, Robinson stands amidst fourteen Aborigines, three dogs (two very English-looking), and a wallaby. His left hand is raised as if in instruction, while his right clasps the hand of an Aboriginal man who in his turn places a reassuring left hand on the shoulder of a fierce warrior who holds a spear and stares not at Robinson, but at the Aboriginal conciliator. Duterrau has painted connection and interdependency. What he saw, and painted for us to see, got lost as the confines of representation closed in upon Trugernanna, marking her out as 'the last', limiting her story to full-stop.

The dynamic inter-connectedness of *The Conciliation* is absent from the photographs of Trugernanna sitting for the camera, from the skeleton in its display case, from the figure frozen in the diorama. In 1978 Tom Haydon returned to Trugernanna as the subject of a film documentary he called *The Last Tasmanian*. A century had passed since Trugernanna's bones had been separated from their flesh in the coffin buried within the ironically protective space of the female factory, and thirty years since the skeleton was removed from display in the museum – and yet here was the same narrative stuck in the same groove. Increasingly, however, the symbolic politics circulating around Trugernanna made people angry or at least uneasy. As the critic Tom O'Regan put it, 'the film leaves no place for the claims of the Tasmanians' descendants to their own separate identity and authentic Aboriginal culture'. Although I doubt whether anyone would dispute that claim today, at least not in public, Trugernanna herself remains caught in the discredited narrative. 'The experience of colonialism', Ian Anderson has said, 'is to fragment and dismember. To resist the colonial project is to reconnect or to make whole.' Trugernanna and William Lanne were dismembered. Those barbaric deeds we cannot undo. What we can re-member are the narratives through which their lives are told, the narratives which connect us back to their world and forward to the world we want to live in. 'Of Trucaninni', wrote a journalist the day after her death, 'we shall no doubt hear many interesting narratives now that she has departed this world'. I hope so.

henry reynolds

ON FIRST LOOKING INTO

RUSDEN'S HISTORY

I CAN REMEMBER MY SURPRISE even now although it was thirty years ago that I first read G.W. Rusden's three-volume *History of Australia* published in 1883. At the time I was beginning to work on the history of Aboriginal–European relations and was reading widely among the literature of the various Australian colonies in the hope that I could develop some understanding of the development of an historiographical tradition prior to the twentieth century.

Unlike many of the authors I had read I knew about Rusden in advance. He had been execrated by the historians of the 1950s and 1960s for his reactionary views and his involvement in the conflict between the upper and lower houses of the Victorian parliament. Melbourne University's Professor R.M. Crawford declared that Rusden imposed his almost ludicrously conservative bias on everything he related. His colleague, A.G. Austin, described him as the elderly conservative who wrote the reactionary history of Australia. For Geoff Searle Rusden was a member of a Victorian 'governing class' who saw themselves as a 'colonial aristocracy' who were completely untouched by the democratic sentiment of the age.

So I knew what to expect – or rather I thought I did. I assumed that Rusden would be an extreme racist, that such views would necessarily accompany his elitist, anti-democratic, high tory stance in colonial politics.

Nothing could have been further from the truth. The elderly conservative turned out to be a passionate defender of the Aborigines and of the Maoris as well. He saw himself as following in the tradition of the great sixteenth-century priest Las Cassas to whom he dedicated his 1888 volume *Aureretanga: Groans of the Maoris*. Like the Spaniard before him he had 'laboured in the cause of humanity'. As I read more about Rusden and of the way readers had reacted to his *History* I realised that others had seen those aspects of the work which had apparently not struck the post-war historians. In a paper on 'Colonial Historical Research' delivered to the 1911 Congress of the Australasian Association for the Advancement of Science, Professor G.C. Henderson of Adelaide University observed that Rusden's trilogy was the only comprehensive history of Australia that was based on the perusal of original and reliable material. But it was, he argued, 'vitiated from beginning to end by the author's determination to prove that the aborigines were victimised by rapacious politicians and squatters'. So strong was Rusden's passion that Henderson believed that his work was not history at all but a 'brief extending over 2000 pages'.

So what was the substance of this brief?

As a young man Rusden had managed pastoral properties and had lived and worked alongside Aboriginal guides and stockmen. As a result of this experience he gained insight into Aboriginal society and came to appreciate its qualities. The tribespeople's 'loyalty to their laws and mutual kindness to one another' could put to the blush many of their white detractors. In a book first published in 1851 and written 'under impression fresh and youthful' he referred to the Aboriginal stockmen who had worked with him:

> I would fain do honour to those artless qualities which have often been my sole social amusement when, week after week, I have sojourned in the bush, with no other companion than my faithful Australian, my dog, and my horse; and I bear willing testimony to the fidelity and cheerfulness which have sometimes made me think my sable companion a pattern worthy of imitation by many of his white and contemptuous supplanters.

In a long passage he catalogued the problems which beset the
Aborigines in the wake of settlement and he set them out with
both understanding and passion, explaining to his readers:

> The former life of the scattered tribes of Australia
> quickly became impossible after the English appeared in
> any district. The settlers, for the most part as ignorant of
> the manners and laws of the disinherited race as any
> unmoved denizen of Wapping, were ready to denounce
> it as an encumbering tree which ought to be cut down
> without delay or remorse. Not making allowances for the
> forced impossibility of living their former life, and
> the powerful obstacles to their adoption of a new one, the
> English public soon accepted the local maxim that the
> Australian black was the lowest type of man. It is but
> just to show some of the influences which tended to
> crush him.

I had come across other nineteenth-century writers who
showed a similar capacity for empathy and understanding and
who eschewed the conventional colonial views of the Aborigines but where Rusden parted company with many of them
was in his fierce denunciation of frontier violence and his condemnation of the settlers themselves. He was writing, 120
years ago, what in contemporary Australia has been called
black armband history. In fact his condemnation of colonial
society, his moral outrage, was more pronounced than in any
twentieth-century text. Rusden's *History* is, then, a valuable

corrective to the commonly expressed view that modern historians who write of destruction and dispossession are imposing on people in the past their own views and moral standards. Nothing could be farther from the truth.

The violence of the colonists was a 'great sin' which had accompanied Australian history from the early days of settlement and was still continuing as he wrote. 'But that it has been,' he declared, 'nay, even now is a sin crying aloud to the covering heavens, and the stars the silent witness, can be denied by no one who knows the course of Australian history.' Writing of the pastoral frontier in New South Wales he observed that the rule was to 'inspire terror by slaughter' and then to treat with 'contemptuous sufferance or marked ill usage the remnant of the tribe'. By the time of the Myall Creek massacre and subsequent trial in 1838 public opinion had been debauched by half a century of 'contemptuous and condoned killing of fellow-creatures'. And one of the most important consequences of the prevailing ways of thought was that information about frontier violence was suppressed, whole communities shielded the perpetrators and approved of their bloody work. Rusden felt he had a mission to expose the lies, uncover the hidden evidence, to pronounce the truth. He declared:

> The melancholy fact that those who are ignorant, or wilfully blind, contradict the truth, or deprecate discussion of it in the hope that it, like the blacks, may die out of the land.

Rusden saved his most savage rhetoric for Queensland where violence was coeval with his composition. 'But how does the heart ache,' he announced, to think of the local Aborigines 'throughout those twenty years done to death, and left mangled and stark on the soil of Queensland.' The very air of the northern colony 'reeks with atrocities committed and condoned'. To compare a catalogue of the atrocities would require volumes. In one of his most bitter gibes he declared that even the colonial statistician had fallen in with the prevailing vice, observing that:

> The Registrar General, Mr Henry Jordan, finds no place for the aborigines in his account of the population. In his table of 'causes of death in Queensland', in 1878, 'arranged in the order of degree of fatality', Mr Jordan omitted the rifle.

In writing to the Aborigines Protection Society in London in October 1883 on the eve of publication of the *History of Australia* Rusden observed that he expected 'a howl from some of the Queenslanders' but that he had been compelled to show the world how the natives were treated in the colony.

Why did Rusden write such powerful black armband history? Why did he pursue his brief through 1200 pages? And why was I so surprised that the extreme reactionary in colonial politics turned out to be so radical in race politics? The most immediate answer is that at the time that I read Rusden I assumed that sympathetic engagement with the Aborigines was symptomatic of left-wing, progressive views and that racism lived comfortably with conservatism. But to understand Rusden it was necessary to move beyond these preconceptions of the 1970s.

Rusden was not a democrat. He had a penchant for aristocracy and an hierarchical society. He lamented that none of the Australian colonies had established hereditary aristocracies and, as he believed, enjoyed 'the social grace and nobleness of motive with which an hereditary order adorns a nation'. He was alienated from colonial society. But he had no difficulty in accommodating the Aborigines in his perceived hierarchy. In fact he thought them more admirable than the colonial working class. He observed that 'comparing the savage with only the lower and uneducated European, it would be hazardous to affirm that the black is inferior to the white'. He could respect the Aborigines and show contempt for the lower orders with the one gesture. He believed in social but not racial hierarchies explaining that:

> In shape, in physiognomy, and in disposition there are as wide difference amongst the Australians as amongst the lower and uncultivated class of Europeans, though they escape observation except from those who have acquired intimate knowledge on the spot … and in intelligence, good humour, and loyalty the despised black race often puts to shame the boors among the vaunting Caucasian intruders.

Rusden associated the democratisation of colonial society, the weakening of control by squire and parson, with the upsurge of frontier violence. Commenting on the widespread popular movement in 1838 to pardon the Myall Creek murderers he observed: 'Never was the vulgar error that the voice of the people is the voice of God more perceptible'. When he turned his attention to the violent Queensland frontier he muttered the waspish aside:

> To such base uses may the product of modern civiliza-
> tion be reduced when exempt from the chastening
> influences of religion and of a well ordered society.

It is equally relevant that Rusden was not an Australian nationalist but an Anglophile who lived in both Britain and Australia, a supporter of Imperial Federation. He was therefore, immune from that strong desire of nationalists, then and now, to suppress the unattractive aspects of the past, to avoid the bloodshed and draw a picture of heroic endeavour and commendable achievements.

So my surprise on first looking into Rusden's *History* was understandable. The author's engagement with the Aboriginal cause arose not despite, but because, he was such an Anglophile, such an Imperialist and such a conservative. It was a very important lesson for a young historian to learn that things are often much more complicated than they seem.

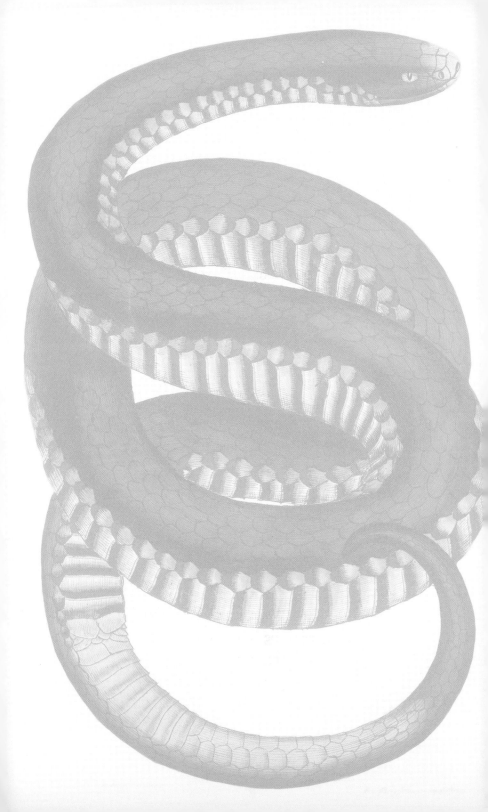

dorothy porter

CALLING A SPADE

FOR BARBARA BAYNTON

There are no ghouls
just gutless human fools.

And too many, depressing thousands
of female mugs
hanging unlovely
from male hooks.

Barbara, thank you,
you took the 'ess'
out of this romantic poetess.

I will never believe again
in the pioneering spirit,
the magnetic ambiguity
of strangers
or the yearning mischief
of a tender blow.

Now if I must portray the bush
he's just a creeping vagrant
who turns snake-nasty at night
with a nose
for a bullied woman.

Only ask mongrel dogs
for love and loyalty.
But no dog's warm muzzle
can nuzzle you to your feet
from the wreck of dumped
and the lying-in-muck
of a broken back.

Forget the solace of nature.
It's a rustling void
that spills into your heart
the drink you will never forget.
Loneliness.
Best drunk chilled.
With a sprig of grime.

IN 1996, at the urging of composer, Jonathan Mills, I read a collection of Australian short stories, set in the bush, written by an author I'd never heard of, Barbara Baynton. Jonathan was keen to write a chamber opera based on one of these stories, 'The Chosen Vessel', and he wanted me to write the libretto. Initially I was reluctant to read *Bush Studies* – the title alone predicted a boring read. I was in for a rude shock. Because shock is what Baynton does best. It would be an understatement to say she is the least sentimental writer I have read. She is shocking. She sends a blistering voltage through the colonial bush yarn. Nothing emerges without terrible black scars. She leaves the romance of mateship, the pioneering spirit and, unforgettably, the shoulder-to-shoulder rural marriage, in smouldering ruins. The Baynton landscape is bleak and terrifying. There are no pantheistic raptures. Its human characters are a mostly unsympathetic mix of vulnerable lonely women and brutish violent men. There are occasional moments of grace and raw courage, usually involving love between woman and child or woman and loyal dog, never between men and women. I eventually wrote the libretto for Jonathan's opera, *The Ghost Wife*, based on Baynton's story 'The Chosen Vessel'. It would have been gutless to have declined. At its best Baynton's work insists on not shirking a challenge, but with eyes wide open and a steady, undaunted gaze.

rodney hall

SUCH IS LIFE: THE MASTERPIECE THAT MIGHT HAVE CHANGED OUR LITERATURE

IN 1957 *VOSS* OPENED a whole new territory to the imagination. The passion and daring of the idea, the grandeur of its scope and the seriousness of the language all amounted to a revelation. So these were the heights Australian fiction could aspire to! Patrick White had raised the bar for all of us. And retrospectively, once we came to read them, *The Aunt's Story* and *The Tree of Man* confirmed the fact.

Half a century earlier a similarly remarkable breakthrough

might have happened. But oddly enough it didn't. *Such is Life*, completed in 1897, was issued finally in 1903 after massive cuts (nearly 400 pages) had been made by the editor to reduce its bulk in the interests of accessibility. Without success, because the resulting book made very little impact. Joseph Furphy's daring masterpiece never quite appealed. Although much of the excised material was eventually published in 1905–6, serialised in the Broken Hill *Barrier Truth*, these parts did not become available between hard covers until after the author's death. Other writers, ignoring what made it so remarkable, doggedly admired its realist detail, its humour and bush characters … any and everything except its astonishingly daring structure.

(The depth of this literary tragedy might be gauged by imagining *Riders in the Chariot* confined to being published solely as episodes in a Broken Hill newspaper.)

Later, during the 1950s, Furphy's great ruin of a novel became something of an icon for the dominant realist school, though, it has to be said, still not widely read. Why, during this resurgence of low-level interest, did it still not liberate other novelists from the strictures of plot and incarceration in dated British notions of 'good writing'? Well, it did not. When they did look to *Such is Life* it was only for confirmation of worthy but conservative working-class storytelling. His name was linked with that of Henry Lawson in this regard, but Lawson was the true star in the firmament, accorded a state funeral even though he had fallen from grace with his alcoholism and turncoat toadying to England.

Having been one of the guilty ones, as a young man in my twenties, and a member of the Realist Writers' Group in Brisbane, I should know. When *Voss* shook us to the core, in many cases shaking us free, we wondered in private how we had come to sink in 'the desolate bog of fifth-rate tales' (as William Gosse Hay put it in the 1930s). Imagine my surprise – I cannot speak for the others – when, at forty, I took up *Such is Life* again and discovered what a masterpiece we had been missing. The fate of Furphy's extraordinary book appears, at least on the surface, to be an enigma and the relative neglect it has suffered arguably the greatest oddity in Australian literary history.

How is it possible that this gloriously inconsequential, learned and earthy masterpiece was sidelined ever since it was first published? And still is? Sidelined, despite many reprintings (including an edition from Jonathan Cape in London in 1936 and another, shortly afterwards, from the University of Chicago Press) and despite inclusion on just about every Australian literature course ever devised? The unavoidable fact is that it has failed to secure a place in the public imagination. There never was the slightest chance of a state funeral for Furphy.

My answer lies partly in the demands *Such is Life* requires of its reader, but mostly in the fact that it does not address the people it speaks about. Though the story concerns ordinary working people in the bush, Furphy never much appealed to them. He spoke about them and for them, but not exactly to them. And they are the ones who made a place in their hearts for Lawson and Paterson. He was more like an advocate for them to others. So, who *was* he addressing? I'd suggest it was a new breed, at the turn of the twentieth century, a distinctively Australian class of intellectual, perhaps best described as sophisticated ockers. And this may well have been the first book to address them specifically. So, while he assumed a sturdy anti-Imperial stance, an interest in the common folk and bush lore, a wide acquaintance with English literature and at least a smattering of the history of philosophy, he also set out to present the narrow society of the rural worker – with the greatest respect and affection – to the wider world of a well-read but sympathetic audience.

Put it this way: these days this well-read but sympathetic audience is rather more likely to have tackled *Ulysses* or *The Life and Opinions of Tristram Shandy*. *Such is Life*, which shares qualities with both them, seems not to have entered the collective awareness of what it is to be Australian, what it is to be addressed familiarly by one of our own.

Yet the Australianness is absolute. The book is funny, at times hilariously funny. The characters are ordinary people: working bullock drivers, shepherds, squatters and farmers of the Riverina district. Tom Collins, Furphy's narrator, establishes a quintessentially Australian tone right from the opening sentence: 'Unemployed at last!'

And his compassionately mocking tone never lets up. Within a few pages Collins buys a stallion. The seller explains that the horse's name is Cleopatra, to which Collins reponds affably: 'A very good name too, I should be sorry to change it.' And he never does change it. Though often, afterwards, 'Men of clerkly attainments took me aside and kindly pointed out what they conceived to be a blunder.'

Tom Collins is a Deputy Assistant Sub-Inspector with a minor public service department, touting a certain K around the district for various persons to fill out (it all begins to sound Kafkaesque), who begins by contemplating his diaries stacked on the table before him: 'Twenty-two consecutive editions of Letts Pocket diary with one week in each opening.' Of course, describing every incident alluded to in every volume would be an impossibly arduous task. So, he explains, he will confine himself to selected samples, fleshing out the events of a single week, in whichever diary he lights upon at random, at whatever page falls open in his hand. This turns out to be the week beginning Sunday, 9 September 1883. And for the next fifty pages he sticks to his task with a huge slab of comic dialogue, which mostly takes place around a campfire and involves the drivers of a number of bullock teams. The bullocks, unhitched from their yokes, have been set free to graze, unauthorised, as trespassers on private pasture while the men relax, exchange news and speculate on the meanings of life.

An important feature of this dialogue is that everything they say is crammed with dashes in place of swear words, to mark Furphy's mocking and inventive use of the bowdlerising conventions of the time, in which even the word *bloody* was not permitted in print. The following brief extract will convey the flavour. One of the bullockies, the foul-mouthed Price, 'qualifying every word that would bear qualification' clears his throat:

'Them misforcunes was invidiously owin' to yer own (adj.) misjudgment,' he said dogmatically.

'Serve you right for not havin' better luck,' added Dixon.

'Learn you more sense, anyhow,' remarked Mosey.

'Misforcunes does some people good,' hazarded Bum.

'Did you count my (bullocks)?' demanded Dixon.

'O you sweet speciment!' retorted Mosey, as he picked up his second yoke. 'Why the (compound expletive) don't you rouse roun'? I got the screwmatics in my (adj.) hip.'

There is no action to speak of. For fifty pages all that can be said to have happened, basically, is that the teamsters break down a fence to get access to forbidden grass and water for their beasts. And they talk. They talk brilliantly, inventively and inexhaustibly. 'Anyhow, interposed Price, it was raining like (incongruous comparison) when I drawed up at the store; an' Moriarty he fetches me inter the office, an' gives me a stiffener o' brandy. Or Whisky? Now, (hair-raising imprecation) if I don't disremember which.'

The talk is rich in stories and character, encompassing a complete society with its values and manners intact. Later in the novel we find, in similar circumstances, that only a lazy bullocky can hope to escape arrest, rousing himself after the police ambush is all over – thus providing an example recognisable to all true patriots.

Chapter Two begins with a disclaimer. Tom Collins has already changed his mind. If he sticks to the promised plan of confining himself to a single week he will also find himself confined to the same cast of bullockies and, in those days of painfully slow travel, the same stretch of territory (a week in camp has significantly fewer possibilities than a day in Dublin). So, he declares, his revised intention is to give us one entry per month, moving straight from 9 September to 9 October 1883, and so forth, 'The thread of the narrative being thus purposely broken, no one of these short and simple analyses can have any connection with another – a point on which I congratulate the judicious reader and the no less judicious writer; for the former is thereby tacitly warned against any expectation of plot or denouement, and so secured against disappointment, whilst the latter is relieved of the (to him) impossible task of investing prosaic people with romance, and a generally haphazard economy with poetical justice.'

Meanwhile, 9 October brings the benefit of his meeting a hapless Irishman, Rory O'Halloran, who: 'regaled me with the folk-lore of the hill-side where his ancestors had passively resisted extinction since the time of Japhet … and legends wherein the unvarying motif was a dazzling cash advance made by Satan in pre-payment for the soul of some rustic dead-beat'. When the time comes for the two men to part, Collins explains how he set Rory up in suitably Australian style and got him started in the morning: 'I gave him my Shakespear as a keepsake, with a billy and pannikin, and a few days' rations. I made up his swag as he lay broken-hearted on his bunk; then I walked him to the Echuca road. So he sorrowed his way northward … and, as I watched his diminishing figure, I prayed that he might be enticed into the most shocking company in Echuca, and be made fightably drunk, and fall in for a remembersome hammering, and get robbed of everything, and be given in charge for making a disturbance, and wind up the adventure with a month in her Majesty's jail.'

Following this new, monthly, structure Collins finds himself (in the grand tradition of comedy) obliged to confess a most embarrassing, personal incident. Reluctantly he explains how the troubles of this day, Friday, 9 November, began with having to swim across a river. He recounts how he reacted to the inconvenience equably enough, stripping off his clothes, folding them and strapping them to his head with an elastic belt, the ends of which he secured between clenched teeth. Then, swimming out into the current, he called [sic] to his enthusiastic dog, Pup, to follow. Pup, a gangling kangaroo dog, joyfully launches himself in pursuit, landing right on the package and nearly drowning his master. The clothes, of course, were lost. The ensuing scene is brilliantly sustained, culminating in incendiarism. Rather than be seen naked, Collins burns down a hayrick as a diversionary tactic while he steals a pair of trousers from some farmer's clothesline.

Even while *Such is Life* digresses, backtracks and gives way to sprawling loquacities bursting with life, the characters reveal themselves through dialogue. They talk and talk and talk: 'Vandemonian Jack, aged about a century, was mechanically sawing firewood in the hot, sticky sunshine. This is one of the jobs that it takes a man four or five score years to perform ungrudgingly.' … 'Mrs Beaudesart, the housekeeper, was well-born. Don't study that expression too closely, or you'll get puzzled. Her father, Hungry Buckley, of Baroona – a gentleman addicted to high living and extremely plain thinking – had been snuffed-out by apoplexy, and abundantly filled a premature grave, some time in the early 'sixties, after seeing Baroona pass, by foreclosure, into the hands of a brainy and nosey financier. People who had known the poor gentleman when he was very emphatically in the flesh, and had listened to his palaver, and noticed his feckless way of going about things, were not surprised at the misfortune that had struck Buckley. Mrs B. had then taken a small villa, near Sydney, where, in course of time, her son and daughter took positions of vantage, such as their circumstances allowed; each being prepared to stake his or her gentility (an objectionable word, but it has no synonym; and nasty things have nasty names) against any amount of filth that could be planked down by an aspiring representative of the opposite sex.' … 'Priestly, a bullock driver, was … a decent enough vulgarian, but altogether too industrious to get any further forward than the extreme tail-end of his profession. Some carriers never learn the great lesson, that to everything there is a time and season – a time for work, and a time for repose … Such a man finds himself born into trouble, as the sparks fly in all directions. The fact is, that the Order of Things is not susceptible of coercion whatever, and must be humoured in every possible way … Priestly, in consequence of being always at work, could get very little work done; and, being pursuantly in a chronic state of debt and destitution, he got only the work that intermittently slothful men wouldn't take at the price.'

Furphy himself had worked as a bullock driver, indeed he owned two bullock teams which he was very proud of, besides having been a farmer and a goldminer. Out there, on the track, among the very working men and women he wrote about, he jotted down ideas in his notebook, ideas that might have astonished his companions into exclaiming, 'What the (sheol) ...!': 'The Spartans (so ran my reflections) were as much addicted to dirt as the Sybarites to cleanliness. The conquering races of later ages – Goths, Huns, Vandals, Longobards, &c – were no less celebrated for one kind of grit than for the other. It is the Turkish bath that made the once-formidable Ottoman Empire the sick man of Europe ... Bathing did the business for Italy ... in the ruins of the fatal Roman baths, the innumerable *strigulae*, used by the bathers to polish their skins, bear sad testimony to the suicidal cleanliness of that doomed race.'

He shares, of course, many of the blindnesses of the period – notably racial prejudice against the Chinese. And his reference to young Australian women as typically having moustaches has led to some unpopularity, though this is part of such slender plot as there is: a clue. The clue being to the identity of Nosey Alf, who turns out to be a woman disguised as a man. She gets away with it thanks to her putative moustache.

In one sense Furphy's mission rather parallels that of

Melville in *Moby Dick*. He seeks connections. Connections between the characters and their situation in life, connections with the wider community, connections with the great traditions of literature, and connections within a metaphysical awe at the richness, the variety of the natural world and of human society.

The current distaste for any polemical element in fiction (as if there ever was such a weird beast as the 'pure' novel) no doubt counts against him. He delights in polemics. He glories in argument and in parading his biases. On just about every issue raised or even implied in this great tirade he has an opinion and nothing will do but he must air it: 'The Church quibbles well, and palters well, and, in her own pusillanimous way, means well, by her silky loyalty to the law and the profits, and by her steady hostility to some unresisting personification known as the Common Enemy ... And whilst the world's most urgent need is a mission of sternest counsel and warning, from the oppressed to the oppressor, I witness the unspeakable insolence of a Gospel of Thrift, preached by order of the rich man to Lazarus.' ... '[Oliver Wendell] Holmes ... denounces witchburning and Inquisition-persecution, like the chivalrous soul that he is ... but ... he has achieved the distinction of being the only American poet of note who blandly ignores slavery, and takes part with the aristocrat, as against the lowly.'

The reader is just lulled into believing the new monthly structure will hold good for the rest of novel when the author declines to deal with what happened on 9 March 1884 and chooses to finish on the 29th instead, a vagary which immediately follows Chapter Six, the great glory of the book, a conversation between Collins and a youngish boundary rider with a severely disfigured face, Nosey Alf.

Repeatedly raising one hand to mask the missing nose and mutilated cheek, Nosey Alf speaks of poetry and love while Collins delves into his vast store of wit to come up with deliciously funny asides. The combination is uniquely Furphy's and provides the novel with a tender and tragic climax because, as every attentive reader will have deduced by now, this boundary rider is not what he seems. The clinching clue comes when we are told the good side of his face is 'more beautiful than a man's face is justified in being' and that, his faint moustache being unnoticeable but for its dark colour, he has no need to shave. This is none other than Warrigal Alf Morris's fiancée, jilted long ago when a horse kicked her in the head, now living in disguise. From the unsuspecting narrator she learns that her lover is still alive and, as a widower, living alone. Her own loss grows intolerable the more she hears.

Collins, himself moved, pulls out his jew's-harp. 'It is not the highest class of music, I am well aware.' And discovers his limited, halting repertoire lifted to a new level by the feelings he shares with the boundary rider. 'How sweetly everything sounds tonight: Bee-o-buoy-bee-o-buoy-bee-o-buoy.' Nosey Alf then offers to reciprocate by playing the violin and does so superbly.

After a hilarious, thousand-word disquisition on music as a mechanism of sound-waves, the narrative returns us to the conversation on the boundary, which turns to poetry and whether there is a difference between men's and women's poetry. Nosey Alf asks to be told what is the mark of women's work. 'Sincerity, I replied. Notwithstanding Mrs. Hemans.'

When Alf sings simple songs with unfaltering purity and a surprising depth of melancholy passion, Collins urges him/her to give up the rural life and go to the city, 'gifted as you are. Maestros, and high-class critics; and other unwholesomely cultured people, might possibly damn you with faint praise; but you could afford to take the chance of that, for beyond all doubt, the million would adore you.'

Funny, erratic and inventive, who cares that his phonetically spelt dialogue is often irritatingly difficult to decode? Yet there was a price to be paid. His gorgeously ornate English made an oddity of him until, in the 1960s, Patrick White achieved a mannered musicality of language capable of exploring the most intense insights. In the intervening sixty years only the almost-forgotten William Gosse Hay, mentioned earlier, had followed a comparable line of inventive and ornate language in *The Escape of the Notorious Sir William Heans*, attempting to break free of the doctrine of art as a mere mirror of the world.

But, essential to Furphy's combination of a verbally florid style with absolute realism of observation is the informed, personal, mocking yet tolerant voice of the narrator. Easy to detect eighteenth-century echoes, of Henry Fielding in particular. I suspect that most of us who love *Such is Life* love it especially for this. The odd thing about it is that for many people the title brings to mind only two things: first, that splendid opening sentence and, secondly, a mistaken notion that the title itself has something to do with Ned Kelly's memorable use of the same popular phrase.

Instead, what it should bring to mind is a rich store of associations as the first Australian novel we can justly call a masterpiece.

So now, friend, like Furphy's hero-narrator – hoping like (sheol) to have inspired you to read, or re-read, this wonderful (far-fetched adj.) book written a hundred years ago by a poor, unjustly neglected (person) – it only remains for me to sign myself off, Tom Collins style, from the Central Office of Unconsidered Trifles:

> *I am, Sir, Madam,*
> *Ynnnnnnnnnnlnny,*
> *MMMnnynnlnny*

bill gammage

MRS AENEAS GUNN

WHO WOULD HAVE PICKED a woman as Australia's most popular writer on the outback? A tiny woman, five-foot-nothing, who spent only fourteen months in the bush, on Elsey Station in 1902–3. She loved it, and wrote two books about it, *The Little Black Princess* (1905) and *We of the Never-Never* (1908). They've sold a million copies so far, most to or for Australian children. Mrs Gunn's Aboriginal 'daughter', Bett-Bett, was imaginary friend to generations of girls, and at my school, boys echoed a long, mournful 'Maluuuka!' to warn of a teacher coming.

Mrs Gunn appealed to teachers. She was one, and she wrote brilliantly on the Elsey men and their speech. Here's the Head Stockman passing time with an angry bull:

There was the sapling bending like a weeping willow, and there was the stag underneath it, looking up at me and asking if he could do anything for me, taking a poke at me boot now and then, just to show nothing would be no bother; and there was me, hanging on to the sapling, and leaning lovingly over him, telling him not to go hanging around, tiring himself out on my account; and there was the other chaps – all lightweights – laughing fit to split, safe in their saplings.

The trouble with saplings, the Head Stockman decided, is 'The farther up you climb, the nearer you get to the ground'.

The Maluka, the Sanguine Scot, the Quiet Stockman, the Dandy, the Fizzer and the rest are all of that mould. They are knights: strong, chivalrous, independent, resourceful, loyal to mates, larger than life, differing from Camelot's knights only in wearing less, caring for their horses better, and not stoushing passers-by. Mrs Gunn drew them so well that they ceased to be bushmen and became 'characters'. Their emerging from the little Missus' pen pinned them forever to her pages. Pinned her too. Born Jeannie Taylor, married less than fifteen months, Mrs Aeneas Gunn she is still.

And pinned the Never Never. Before Mrs Gunn, 'never never', like 'outback', skittered wraithlike just beyond advancing white settlement. The Northern Territory did not own it: there was no Northern Territory in 1902 – it was part of South Australia. *The Australian National Dictionary* has 'never

never' meaning outback New South Wales in 1833, and an 1857 use stemming from a Kamilaroi (NSW) word for remote parts. *The Dictionary of New Zealand English* cites it used there in the Australian sense in 1908, the year *We of the Never-Never* was published. 'Outback' still skitters about, but Mrs Gunn anchored 'never never' to the Northern Territory forever.

She championed Aborigines. Sometimes she called them 'niggers', and she would have been surprised that they own Elsey Station now. But she condemned the killing times, she admired Aboriginal bushcraft and care for each other, and she knew the Elsey mob, mostly Yangman people, well enough to get the drift of their totemic system. 'The blacks are very wonderful', she wrote,

> To have any idea of how wonderful they are, you
> must live among them, going in and out of their
> camps, and having every one of them for a friend.
> Just living in a house that happens to be in a
> blackfellow's country is not living among blacks,
> although some people think it is.

But she was a visitor. She had barely settled in when an old resident, malarial dysentery – blackwater fever – killed her husband, ended her days of enchantment, and sent her back to Melbourne and nearly sixty years of widowhood. She wrote in grief for a lost husband and a lost world, widow to both, her heart at the Elsey. She saw the vision splendid, then lost it for-ever, as in all great chivalric tales.

At least one of her knights killed Aborigines, plenty of them, and might still have been killing in 1902. Mrs Gunn must have glimpsed that, must have wondered on that day when the Elsey men fired their revolvers in the air and every black man, woman and child in earshot, even Bett-Bett, took to the bush, and stayed hidden for hours. She said nothing. At least until 1916 Elsey's Aborigines were being killed, and helping to kill people further north.

She missed other things too. She did not have a good eye for country. Look at her maps. And what trees were about Elsey homestead, what grasses? These questions matter for cattle, but she doesn't say. She mentions 'white gum'; bloodwood and spear grass dominate the old site. Good cattle country if you keep burning it, but hot, dry, termite mound country. No wonder Jeannie loved to get up to Bitter Springs and the Roper River.

What cattle breeds did the Elsey run? How many head were on its one and a quarter million acres? She doesn't say. She does say the run needed two hundred horses a year, which might mean four or five thousand cattle. Or it might not, for her husband began as a sheep man. In 1890 he and his cousin Joseph Bradshaw, both to become fellows of London's Royal Geographical Society, took up Gunn's Spring on the Prince Regent River in the Kimberleys, and stocked it with 4000 sheep. They abandoned it in 1895 and took up Bradshaw's Run on the Victoria River, but they kept the sheep. The Elsey was the Maluka's first go at cattle.

She doesn't say much about horses either. Horses filled

the lives of the Elsey men. She depicts only one vividly. She has fine sketches of the Quiet Stockman horse-breaking and the Fizzer dry-staging his carefully chosen team, but she also acknowledges the 'minute exactness' of correspondents in providing her with such technical detail.

She wasn't writing for people who wanted to know these things. She was writing what it felt like: big, wonderful, egalitarian, free, with people to suit, almost all of them men, Anzacs in the making. It is not surprising that she later devoted herself to returned soldier causes, and that the Victorian RSL honoured her for it.

Anzac was not the only change coming. In 1902 the Elsey straddled a crossroads. Leichhardt, Gregory and McDouall Stuart had all passed through, and in 1856 Gregory named the creek after John Ravenscroft Elsey, his surgeon and naturalist, who died the next year, aged twenty-four, thus initiating a melancholy custom for men connected with the Elsey. The run was the third in the Top End to be established, in 1881. In 1902 it had so many visitors because nearby the overland telegraph, guiding travellers south-north, crossed the main stock route from Western Australia. The stock route followed water north from the Kimberleys, swung east and south in a giant arc to the Roper, on Elsey land north of the homestead, then turned east along Leichhardt's track, across the bottom of the Gulf into Queensland.

It was not a good route. Too long. In the good season of 1904 Blake Miller with 1100 Kidman cows pioneered the Murranji Track, 125 miles from Top Springs east to Newcastle

Waters. The Murranji was dangerous. Water was uncertain, and the track threaded through lancewood and bulwaddy scrub. Cattle would edge behind trees and stand quietly hoping to be missed – you had to watch all ways all the time. If cattle rushed, in a trice the scrub could skewer man or beast or scrape off a rider. You could lose half a mob no trouble. Until road trains put an end to the droving game in the 1960s, the Murranji was the supreme test of the drover, but it saved 600 miles. It ran south-west of the Elsey, and it let the station's new owners shift the homestead north onto the old route on the Roper, in 1905–6. It also led the government to put bores across the Barkly Tableland. The main Queensland stock route then moved well south, following the Mitchell and Flinders grass plains to the railheads beyond Camooweal and Lake Nash. The Elsey was bypassed.

Death changed the Elsey too. In the decade after the Maluka died, six of Jeannie's knights followed him to the grave. At least two died chivalrously. Jock McPhee, Tam-O-Shanter, died of thirst trying to save a sick tracker on the Murranji in 1910. Henry Ventlia Peckham, the Fizzer, drowned crossing Campbell Creek on the Victoria River in 1911, trying to get help for a sick woman. Most of the rest were dead within thirty years. The last was the Quiet Stockman, the one who kept clear of women, who had six children before he died at Angaston, South Australia, in 1960.

In 1944 one of those in Mrs Gunn's spell, Brigadier E.M. Dollery, commanding NT Force, decided to restore Elsey Cemetery and bury all her 'characters' in it. He got Jeannie's support. She was grateful that her husband's grave would be repaired. No-one had touched it since the Fizzer erected the plaque and the posts and rails she had sent from Melbourne forty years before. In September 1944 the Fizzer was re-buried beside his handiwork. Then came Happy Dick, the Wag, and the Sanguine Scot. 'Bush-folk have long memories and love to rest now and then beside the milestones of the past', Jeannie wrote in one of her most memorable phrases, but only three of Elsey Cemetery's fourteen graves are known with certainty.

Two Cemetery monuments are to characters buried elsewhere. The last of the Elsey mob to die, both were women: Jeannie Gunn, and Dolly Bonson. 'When she wants to be very important,' Jeannie wrote, 'we have to call her "Dolly", her whitefellow name, she says.' She said right. Her father, Louis Cummings, christened her that in 1892. She died in Darwin on 8 March 1988, aged ninety-five, eighty-six years after Aeneas, twenty-seven after Jeannie. Through all those years she lived in thousands of minds and hearts as Bett-Bett, the Little Black Princess, her growing up as vivid as any in Australian literature. Lived in the sense Peter Pan did: because readers imagined her. If they didn't she vanished, for through all those years she remained determined to be Dolly. Only she was truly at home in the Never Never; only she refused to become one of the Little Missus' characters.

beverly farmer

COONARDOO: THE WELL IN THE SHADOW

TO SET A SCENE: 1961, I've got my degree and at twenty I'm finally at a loose end, having spent years breaking all my ties to family, country, class, culture. I've grown up convinced only stunted lives are lived in Australia. Not that I care any more. Words have failed me. I've gone from being someone who lived in and for books from earliest childhood to someone who can hardly bring herself to open a book. I can only sneer inwardly – the voices of the English Department in my ears – at the passion for books which took me so eagerly off to university as the ideal training ground for a writer (wanting) to be.

Now my sights are set on Europe, where the soil is deep and rich, so I believe – except I'm broke. I'm well and truly staying put. Isn't it time I came down to earth?

Probably. I have a room in a rooming-house and a job in an oyster bar. One night after work, for the first time since my last Ion Idriess a decade earlier, before the syllabus and the booklist, I pick up an Australian novel: Xavier Herbert's *Capricornia*. It's broadly splashed on a wide canvas, passionate, scornful, riproaring stuff, and to my surprise I love every word. It's that as much as anything – the familiar way with words, the feel of the tongue in the ear and mouth – the *Sprachgefühl* – that salt of the Australian earth.

Encouraged, I move on to an earlier book with a similar setting, Katharine Susannah Prichard's *Coonardoo*. This is recognisably the same world as *Capricornia* and the characters are virtually interchangeable, though here the women take up the foreground. *Coonardoo* is on a different scale, smaller and tighter, less robust, with a physicality so glossed over that it reads a lot like romance fiction. In short, where *Capricornia* is salt, *Coonardoo* is honey, and I'm on my guard, sniffing a *Women's Weekly* plot. But I'm wrong. This romance is tragic, in the high European tradition of baulked and fatal loves. And for all the lyricism, as an outback saga it goes even further than *Capricornia* because the heroes are the black characters, the underclass, the dying race.

And, what's more, this white woman dared to cast a lubra, a gin, a bit of black velvet, alongside a white man. One of the *Bulletin* judges who gave *Coonardoo* the 1929 novel prize, while praising her style and sensitivity to the landscape, had to protest. It said a lot for her power of imagination that KSP (as she signed herself) could even conceive of a romantic heroine who was black, and as for pulling it off: 'With any other native, from fragrant Zulu girl to fly-kissed Arab maid, she could have done it. But the aboriginal, in Australia, anyway cannot excite any higher feeling than nauseated pity or comical contempt.'

Charming. How did the man in the street feel about it, though, and the woman? And what would have been the reaction if a white woman – Phyllis, let's say, Hugh's daughter – had fallen in love, not with a white stockman with that Laurentian faunish sexiness about him, but an Aboriginal stockman similarly endowed? Did it even cross her mind – KSP's? The love of black velvet was all around her, an open secret, but it stayed sex, by barter or savage force. When it did amount to love, it was never given love's name. You kept your mouth shut. And it never cut both ways. What would have happened to a white woman who loved a black man, openly or in secret? And to the man?

KSP didn't go that far, but she went further in *Coonardoo* than anyone else had. Too far for many, then and now.

I can tell right away this is no masterpiece. I'm well trained, and the makings are all on show. The story is jerky, with jarring changes of key. The dialogue is overdone, like a radio play, heavy-handed. The heroine is a constant angel, much too good to be human. In fact, all the black characters are dealt with scrupulously at arm's length, as if KSP has learned rather than known them, and fears to intrude. Hugh's motivation is too often a blank or, worse, is run through perfunctorily after the event, when disbelief has already snapped taut. So at the climax when he – Hugh! – turns on Coonardoo in a jealous rage and bashes her, drags her through the fire and leaves her for dead, throws her off the land – oh, come on, I think, melodrama, and all in such a vacuum of consequence that he forgets all about it, and so does everyone else! Not Hugh. He couldn't.

Oh, but he could. If not Hugh personally – simply because he's not a fully realised character – then many a man in Hugh's place could and did. What's to stop him? Coonardoo belongs to Wytaliba body and soul. Wytaliba belongs to Hugh.

And are things so different three decades or so further on, in the 60s as I lie reading on a mattress in a Fitzroy slum?

Or so I remember it. Yet the book won't go away: clumsy or not, messy, spindly and knobbly and stripped bare, it stays with me. I think of the first sight of gum trees to those early settlers with eyes nourished on oak and ash and beech: gums with rough trunks or white and smooth or peeling like sunburnt skin, shedding next to no shade on the scatter of bark and twigs and leafblades underfoot, the long-lipped fungi, pods and seeds, beady droppings, feathers, bracken, burrs. The gums are right, though, where they are, you have to see it whole. Seeing only what was awry in *Coonardoo*, have I been missing the wood, the bush, for the trees?

I've seen some for myself by now – not all, and not the

part in *Coonardoo* – in long bouts of hitchhiking and trudging along with my wits about me, bedding down on beaches and in sleep-outs, spare rooms and, at a pinch, prison cells – to be befriended by strangers and pick up new knowledge every day about this country and its way with words. I've seen the same brave white veneer of buildings and stock as Wytaliba at lonely stations out past Broken Hill, with touches like Wytaliba's horses with their 'Dago names', Juno, Ceres, Dionysus: all the hubris and pathos of us in the teeth of a strange land.

Is that why *Coonardoo* is haloed in my memory with a sense of revelation? It's certainly not the sort of revelation *Ulysses* was, a couple of years before, or *To the Lighthouse* will be twenty years on. It isn't what, straight out of university, I would even say was a literary experience, in the main: it isn't as literature that I see it as some sort of revelation and feel my life changing, opening up. More a matter of: *Now is the way clear* … The book fell into my hands when I needed and was ripe for it. It's a dynamic, as reading is at its best. It's like travel in that way, like love at first sight – why *this* book, this person or city? – and it feels like a miracle at the time, and then in retrospect, self-evident.

In her book I've seen the country giving itself to KSP, and her grasping it in both hands. Would it even rate on any scale of the novel to an overseas reader whose gods are Tolstoy, Flaubert, Henry James – someone from Europe? Probably not … unless they lived here. Then they might *see*. Is that it? See what? The country being written down, from scratch. As Russia still is today, after all, and France … However thoroughly written their countries have been by now, it doesn't stop anyone rewriting them today, in the making. And the same raw material – if we are artists, in words, paint, stone, music – is in our hands, and so is what we make of it.

KSP had seen, and got her vision down on paper. Imperfectly. Granted: it's a matter of degree. And so what? – since it got through to me in the end, mutilated but alive, beyond the words, through and before the words – the novel-in-the-mind before the words came to give it body. Which is what's supposed to happen when a book is any good. Of course it does happen all the time, whether or *not* a book is any good: it only takes a reader with an affinity for it. And outside the academy, I realise, this is all to the good.

Elizabeth Hardwick has put it best: 'A certain humility is necessary about the lowly, badly hammered nails if the poor house, completed, moves you to tears … Sometimes literature is not made with words.'

So I came out of a form of bondage. I was back on track, with my nose in books, for the first time in years a general reader, not a student with a mind to meeting the expectations of examiners. I had gone for compliance at first, then rebellion. Now I was free. What I wasn't, surprisingly, was off the hook. It was harder and more demanding when there were no rules and I simply – it slips so glibly off the tongue (what's simple about it?) – had to make up my own mind. Being free meant not choosing to narrow the aperture all over again: not reading a book as a critic, apparatus to the ready – or as a 'woman', or an 'Australian' or a follower of any creed or 'ism'. If something

was worth reading, it was worth a full and fair reading, bringing no less than the whole self to it, every pore open. Not that
the self was a blank page either – but the thing was the
reader's intention to be open to the book and not let anything
come between them.

Meanwhile I'd had a vision of my own. It was a spark,
indivisible, a unity. I took care not to 'unpack' it at the time,
carrying it around close to my chest. I'd put it down when I
could, if I could, but how? Piecemeal, I thought, that's how it's
done. On the one hand, words; on the other, your world of
things to be put into words: and you pieced them together,
trying out the fit sentence by sentence, if it took a lifetime.

All very well, but where did this leave *Coonardoo*?

If it isn't exactly love (what is love, exactly?), I find I'm more
in sympathy with it now. A life story, ending in death, begins
with a child: a happy little girl who was – at least in the 60s –
already familiar under another name to a generation of white
kids who'd found *A Little Black Princess* in their Christmas
stockings. Here's a new Bett-Bett at play in the dust, called
Coonardoo. It means the *well in the shadow*: a real well under
the trees at the blacks' camp at Wytaliba, a cattle station
owned by old Mrs Watt and then her son Hugh – 'You', as the
blacks say. Hugh and Coonardoo are playmates. They grow up
together. She marries. He marries. They never speak their
love's name.

And she is the water of life in a dry land, so that by the
end Coonardoo looms as large as Hardy's Tess over her native

soil, embodying, as Tess does, its innocent abundance; and she too is rejected and left to her fate, a ruined angel. When she staggers, riddled with disease, back to Wytaliba to die where she belongs, she finds it deserted, the homestead falling down, the creek dry, even the dark well almost dry. Why? She is delirious, full of visions. Her people, mourning the loss of her, already understand why. Chitali knows: 'Was she not the well in the shadow? Had she not some mysterious affinity with that ancestral female spirit which was responsible for fertility, generation, the growth of everything? ...'

> Little feet of the kangaroos were doing their devil dance in the twilight. Coonardoo's voice fluttered out; embers of her fire were burning low. Crouched over them, a daze held her. From that dreamy and soothing nothingness, Coonardoo started suddenly. The fire before her had fallen into ashes. Blackened sticks lay without a spark.
>
> She crooned a moment, and lay back. Her arms and legs, falling apart, looked like those blackened sticks beside the fire.

She lays herself down on the earth. And whose doing is this? Hugh's, with the whole thrust of colonial arrogance at his back. All along he has been as helpless as Coonardoo to make sense of the forces at work. Where other white men can, and do, make the most of it, Hugh makes the least. As a character he remains a void – as a man, a nonentity with a kind of blank well-meaningness to him, but blind, stubborn, out of his depth in his own life. Stunted, in fact. A man born and raised into power beyond his means.

Hugh isn't in at the death – having lost Wytaliba to the bank, he's gone prospecting – but he's heard about her downfall. If he understands his own – 'That we are ruined by the thing we kill', as in Judith Wright's poem – there's no sign. Hugh is the husk of a man by now. He's done for. As long as he lives, Coonardoo will be his badge of shame, as he always feared – only not the way he feared.

Having arrived at *Coonardoo* by way of English Literature, one thing I sensed in every pore was the influence, mostly benign, of D.H. Lawrence, whose friend Cynthia Asquith once said that a walk with him 'made you feel that hitherto you had walked the earth with your eyes blindfolded and your ears plugged'. She also wrote in her diary, ineffably, 'He is a Pentecost to one'; and one sees what she meant, fiery on every page of him. KSP certainly did, having read *Sons and Lovers* and fallen under the spell. His spirit flickers all through her Australian bush.

Hers is a different bush from his, though, as she was at pains to point out when *Kangaroo* came out. Lawrence had got it wrong, he hadn't understood what he was seeing. Which is nonsense, of course: he wrote what he saw, with his English eyes – and whatever getting it right is in a work of art, it's not laying down the law on how it's to be seen. It's more like Lily Briscoe in *To the Lighthouse*, standing up for herself, paintbrush in hand, doggedly thinking: 'But this is what I see; this is what I see'.

They had an affinity. Lawrence was KSP's sort of heart-on-sleeve writer, and slapdash where necessary, always choosing life, the wellspring, over form. *He* would have come to fool-hardy grips with any Aboriginal characters he had. He never set eyes on northern Australia and his landscapes are of the south, silvery and ominous: 'Australia has a marvellous sky and air and blue clarity,' he wrote in a letter home, 'and a hoary sort of land beneath it, like a Sleeping Princess on whom the dust of ages has settled.'

Coonardoo will come to mind when I read that sentence, Coonardoo laying herself down, a Sleeping Princess. But long years will go by before I read *Kangaroo* or Lawrence's *Letters* or, for that matter, *To the Lighthouse*.

Going back in time, I've had trouble finding where exactly the book shone forth. It comes in a few short lines at the end, a scrap of dialogue at the parting of Hugh – 'You', as he still is on Wytaliba – from Winni, his son by Coonardoo. In a moment of truth so understated that you'd miss it if you were skimming, Hugh's fall is absolute.

How did KSP pull this off, when it was so far beyond anything else in the book, beyond her reach, perhaps not even reached for, it just fell in her lap – one scrap of dialogue that says everything about Hugh, about Winni, about black and white in Australia. No point even quoting something that takes the whole book to hit home. It's a moment of complete simplicity, no heroics, the plain humanity I was taught to value above rubies in Homer, Shakespeare – *Pray you, undo this button* – and the Norse sagas, without realising it was native to my own country. A brief exchange, stoical and down-to-earth, a vernacular moment that is classical in its restraint: Trojan, Spartan, Icelandic. Australian.

It's like the moment at the end of *To the Lighthouse* where the whole creation, having gathered the momentum of a symphony, poises on one beat as Lily Briscoe puts the last brushstroke on her painting and thinks – *I have had my vision* – and those readers who have been swept along to this resolution know she is speaking for Virginia Woolf as well, and for us, the readers. In the same way I put down *Coonardoo* thinking, *I have had my vision*: knowing, of course, that I've had *her* vision, KSP's, which she has made me feel is mine.

Such visions, revelations, lying dormant like seeds in books. Van Gogh, in a letter not long before he died, wrote how he wanted to do portraits *which would appear to the people of a later century like apparitions*. If portraits in words can do the trick, then the black scarecrow of Coonardoo, a prawners' moll, filthy, gaunt and pox-ridden at the fire, will haunt us. And Hugh did that: who? 'You' did that. 'You' is You, and Me. 'You' is Us.

Coonardoo in its day was an eye-opener, for me and for Australia at large, I hope – 'Australia' as a nation, that creature of the imagination, as unruly and provisional as any individual self. It just takes a while to sink in.

tom griffiths

FLYING FOX AND DRIFTING SAND:

GOING WITH THE FLOW

THE COOPER DISTURBED FRANCIS Ratcliffe. He felt a formless fear there. 'The dry bed of that dead river,' he wrote, '… was one of the most eerie and haunted spots I have ever visited.' He called Cooper's Creek a dead river not only because it did not have water in it when he first saw it in 1935 – it had not flowed in its lower reaches for seventeen years – but also because it could never know the sea. It seemed that it did not have water and never reached water. Even when it did run, it could not fulfil the destiny of a river and release into the ocean. It was dry and landlocked and frustrated. It was a parody of a river. It epitomised the irony, the menace, the waywardness of Australian nature. 'I can never think of the Cooper and the Diamantina as mere rivers,' Ratcliffe reflected. 'They have spirits of their own, which are not friendly to man.'

This anxious Englishman wrote of his fear in *Flying Fox and Drifting Sand*, a book much loved by Australians that was first published in London in 1938, Sydney in 1947, and reprinted many times since. It recounted his two early journeys in Australia, the first in 1929–31 to study fruit bats ('flying foxes') along the eastern coast, and the second in 1935–6 to investigate the causes of soil erosion ('drifting sand') in northern South Australia and south-west Queensland. Ratcliffe was thus exposed to two quite different and challenging environments of Australia – green forest and red desert, the coastal 'jungle' inhabited by an eerie creature, and the vast outback in one of its worst seasons. The book he wrote still sits on homestead shelves in country Australia, probably beside the Bible, Shakespeare and Ion Idriess. Ratcliffe later had a distinguished career as a scientist and conservationist but he is best known for this one book.

Its popularity is in some ways surprising. The book was well written, full of stories, and offered many engaging evocations of nature, but it also contained severe and sobering judgments of the Australian environment and its limited potential for European settlement. Its truths are still resisted by some Australians today.

In contrast to his bracing assessment of the Australian environment, Ratcliffe generously praised Australian people.

Flying Fox and Drifting Sand became popular and beloved because Australians basked in the glow of commendation from a British professional. Although the book was subtitled *The Adventures of a Biologist in Australia*, it was mostly about the tallest vertebrates in the antipodean ecosystem, and especially the exotics, the imported Europeans. 'It was the fineness of the pioneer people of Australia that seems to have been Mr Ratcliffe's most abiding memory of his wanderings', wrote a reviewer in the *Sydney Morning Herald* in March 1938. 'He was the welcome guest of cattle and sheep men, timber-cutters and farmers, spent happy days on holdings which ran past the horizon, in bush clearings, at camps in remote valleys, and came away with an abiding admiration for the qualities of the men and women he there encountered.'

Last year I travelled along the Cooper with Francis Ratcliffe's words, and with his own unsettled spirit. I was interested in the roots of his fear – and his admiration – and in the legacy of his storytelling. Although a lifetime separated our journeys, I travelled much as Ratcliffe had done, as an outsider but staying with the locals, talking science and history along the way, imagining past and future, his book in my swag.

THE DEVIL ON THE WING

When Ratcliffe arrived in Australia in 1929, he knew little of the country, and even less about Australian fauna. He saw everything with new, outsider's eyes. He recorded his delight on first seeing two kookaburras in the Melbourne Botanic

Gardens – 'quite the most loved bird in Australia, and quite the most grotesque'. In Queensland, he found an echidna on a moonlight walk in search of flying foxes, carried it back to camp wrapped in his shirt, and soon observed it in the cooking pot of a couple of bush workers. He was shocked at the market in possum skins in Queensland in 1929, where over a million were expected to be sold in Brisbane in the one month open season. Even the legendary inefficiency of the Queensland railways seemed connected to the exploitation of wildlife. 'I am told,' he wrote home to his family in May 1929, 'that it is quite usual for the train to stop at pubs on the route while the driver and conductor have a drink. More incredible still, the driver keeps a shot gun in the tender, and when he spots a "turkey" [the Great Bustard] in the bush, will pull up the train and get out and stalk it. If the hunt is crowned with success, the bird is handed over to the hotel where he puts up at the end of the journey in part payment of his bill.' 'I have never come across such a nation of bird and animal murderers,' Ratcliffe commented grimly. This language would be echoed almost forty years later when the zoologist Jock Marshall published his angry and feisty collection entitled *The Great Extermination: A Guide to Anglo-Australian Cupidity, Wickedness and Waste* (1966).

On this first trip to Australia, Francis Ratcliffe was employed by the Empire Marketing Board (EMB), an organisation formed in 1926 to mobilise British science for the economic integration of empire; it was the Empire's last hurrah. The EMB embraced an imperial vision in which Australia would play a leading role as an exporter of commodities and a place where British migrants could settle on the land in the yeoman tradition. This was an era of biology as an international economic instrument and tool of empire. In the 1920s the Colonial Office was the main employer of British biologists. It was no surprise, then, that the promising young Ratcliffe finished up at the ends of empire.

He had been brought to Australia to study a 'pest', a native animal. Flying foxes raided, damaged and ate fruit that might have fed the empire's markets, and it was Ratcliffe's job to analyse the problem. Fruit growers saw it as a pest that required extermination. Ratcliffe saw it as his task to get an 'accurate picture of their population as a whole and what might be called their economy'. Ironically, although he'd crossed the world to study them, although he was paid to pursue them, he found it quite difficult – once on the ground – to find them. A couple of months into his trip, Ratcliffe had still only met his beast in the drawers of museum cabinets. 'Flying foxes, unfortunately, seem to be rare …,' he concluded. They were moving north just ahead of him, dispersing into their smaller winter colonies.

Flying fox camps probably represent the largest congregations of land mammals in Australia. A high density roost site may contain over a million foxes. You know they're there from the racket, using over twenty different calls, and from the camp's musky smell. F. Lawson Whitlock, the Western Australian naturalist, described the smell of the flying fox as 'a strong smell which I can only describe as something between over ripe cheese and stale fish. A rather sickly effect it had on me.' Ratcliffe said he could often hear them from a quarter of a mile away, and could smell them from twice as far. Seeing a camp of flying foxes take to the wing, watching these mammals blacken the sky was – still is – one of the great natural experiences of Australia. Ratcliffe never forgot his first observation of this startling phenomenon.

He encountered 'this creature of the jungle' on Tamborine mountain, south of Brisbane, at first a lone individual, quiet and haunting in silhouette, seen 'as a dark shadow sailing across a gap in the trees'. Ratcliffe felt excited, but it was 'not wholly the cool excitement of the scientist', he admitted. 'There was something in it deeper and more disquieting.' In the company of these creatures he often 'had to fight back an uneasy desire for sunlight and human company'. It was a moment reminiscent of the first European encounter with these giant bats, when in 1770 one of Captain Cook's crew at Endeavour River reported seeing a lone creature 'as black as the devil, and had wings; indeed I took it for the devil …'.

But then, over six months into his fieldwork, Ratcliffe had a revelatory experience. One evening as spring advanced, he encountered his beasts in unimaginable numbers at Byfield, just north of Rockhampton in Queensland:

> Then I beheld a miracle. I had walked through the scrub
> that day, and the day before, and, as I said, had been
> hard put to it to get a glimpse of more than a hundred
> or so foxes at a time. Yet from the darkness to my right

the beasts belched forth in thousands – in hundreds of thousands. They rose like smoke from the black tree tops, and after circling once or twice, joined the great column winging its way to the south. As they took to the air the musky smell of their bodies pervaded the little clearing. … It was an altogether unforgettable experience, a natural counterpart, on a colossal scale, of the rabbit from a hat.

'It wrecked all my previous ideas as to large numbers', he wrote. 'I did not believe that there were so many animals in the world.'

By the end of his two years in Australia Ratcliffe 'held out little hope of successful control of the pest'. He bravely concluded that, contrary to general belief, 'the flying fox is not a serious menace to the commercial fruit industry'. The problem was not the species but the behaviour of 'a tiny minority in a huge and mobile population'. Wholesale extermination would be impossible and impractical, although he countenanced some selective slaughter. He admitted that his solution was 'tinged with defeatism'. But it was a radical scientific solution in the sense that it was historical, not technical; it was social, not biological. It demanded that people change, not nature. They had to learn to live with the 'pest'. Furthermore, Ratcliffe concluded that the flying fox population was in fairly rapid decline due to destruction of their habitat. 'You should have come here some years ago', he was continually told, 'then you could have seen the beasts flying over from the coast in such great numbers that the sky was blackened for more than an hour'.

A HALF-CIVILISED CONTINENT

When he first left Brisbane in search of his beasts, he 'had no plan of campaign'. 'I had no idea how long I should be away, or where I should finish up. This is quite the best way of setting out on a journey.' He got around on his motorbike, singing at the top of his voice as he rode. He considered himself 'a lone-wolf worker' but was determinedly social in search of information. He sometimes conducted 'a small-town pub crawl' looking for informants. He allowed himself to be handed around a region by the locals; he steeped himself in regional folklore. Hearsay and memory were, for a while, the main sources of his knowledge about flying foxes. Initially, he had quite some trouble seeing them for himself, shooting them, dissecting them, working with the red, raw material of the scientist. He depended upon the network of informers that he carefully built up, and talked affectionately about 'tickling up the intelligence service'.

It was part of his scientific task, then, to engage with the Australian people and to assess their character. But it was also his instinctive, inherited cultural mission. Ratcliffe was an empire man, an Englishman born in British India who was initially critical of what Australians did to his English language. Francis's father, S.K. Ratcliffe, powerfully shaped his son's imperial vision. S.K. worked in journalism in India and the United

States and was a notable lecturer on BBC radio. His political interests were in British statecraft, decolonisation, the civil service abroad, international agreements and foreign policy: he was, then, a British student of the end of empire. As a commentator on American affairs, he reminded his British public of just what a different country America had become, especially through high immigration: 'the great majority of our fellow countrymen still look upon the US as a stray from the British system, a lost member of the Anglo-Saxon family', he wrote. But they are not quite our kinsmen, he warned: 'You should not think, as many of our people have always thought, that because North America speaks our tongue (in its own way) the people of the US ought to think as we think. That is a delusion.' Through his loyal and frequent letters home, Francis Ratcliffe was in constant dialogue with his father whilst encountering Australia. While Ratcliffe the son was exploring the 'frontier' of Australia, Ratcliffe the father was explaining to Britons the pioneering history of the American West and its contribution to national character. Both were alert to the geographical divergence of British stock, the workings of environment on society.

The younger Ratcliffe's first impressions of Australian society were damning. Observing the country as its economy tipped into depression, he considered the nation's politics 'spiteful and shallow'. He thought that 'the public life of the Australian is about as low a development as civilisation can afford to produce'. 'As far as I can see Australia will be a good place to be out of in a few years time', he concluded, and sometimes he 'wondered why I had left home to chase bats over this half-civilised continent'. On going to Townsville in June 1929, he concluded: 'I think it is now time to retract any of the decent things I have said about Australians'.

Ratcliffe could not help discerning a degeneration of the British race on the Australian frontier. This sensibility was typical of interwar British cultural politics – and science. The Anzac legend, with its celebration of bush vitality and colonial virility, was born to combat it. In June 1929 Ratcliffe was relieved to join a party of English people on a Great Barrier Reef Expedition, a welcome change, as he put it, 'after a dose of concentrated Australia'. He found 'Some indefinable difference between even the pick of the well-educated Australians and these Britishers'. 'They really are a hopeless crowd, are the Australians. At times they fill me with a mingled despair and contempt …'

He was repelled by what he called 'the fundamentally rotten state of Australian politics, which [he said] is the result of the natural independence, arrogance, and selfishness of the native Australian, which seems to rule in all matters except his dealings with his personal friends'. Ratcliffe concluded that 'Unfortunately the independent arrogant spirit of the people precludes the possibility of a Mussolini. If one did appear, I may say, I should be one of the first to put on a black shirt.'

Years later the same people became the heroes of his book. The Cooper helped change his mind.

COOPER DREAMING

Last night we stayed in the most beautiful place imaginable. We unrolled the swags on a gentle knoll beside Cooper's Creek. It was at the Cullyamurra Waterhole, the deepest in the system, the place which has the largest peak flow of any river in Australia. Just above the waterhole is 'the choke' where the flare of the Cooper channels narrows, and there – above a floodline on the rocks – is an Aboriginal quarry and gallery, every boulder an artefact, every rockface a canvas. It's worth remembering that Burke and Wills died not of heat and thirst in the middle of nowhere, but of malnutrition, exhaustion, thiaminase poisoning (from raw nardoo) and the cold (Burke accidentally set fire to their wurley and burnt most of their spare clothes) in a watered and inhabited place of art and industry.

Large graceful coolibahs spread their limbs above us, and the creek was a chortle of bird noise, especially the grunting and grinding of pelicans as they sailed the waters majestically or flew in formation or glided in to land on the pond like Hercules bomber aircraft. There were egrets, and pacific herons and night herons and hardhead ducks and black kites. After the big wet earlier this year, the banks of the Cooper were green with native spinach, with which we supplemented our evening campfire meal. It was delicious – and ironic, too, to live off the land even in this small way in a setting of such European hopelessness. There was a sense of such abundance, of rippling waters, dense bird life, bush tucker, an inland Eden, and yet it was here that Burke and Wills perished. Without any doubt they spent their last weeks near our campsite, would have walked over it several times. The Yantruwanta people brought the explorers food every day, looking after them tenderly, but Burke knocked the nets of fish out of their hands and ordered King to fire over their heads because he was 'afraid of being too friendly'.

As night closed in, I read aloud two chapters of Alan Moorehead's account of the expedition, *Cooper's Creek*. It was haunting and eerie to read it there, around a campfire on the Cooper, to learn of their despair, their camel swallowed by the mud, their hopeless chasing of branches of the waterhole, looking for a watered route out, knowing that they dragged their feet over this very ground, under these trees, stared at this sky. A place of such beauty and capricious bounty needs only an epic tragedy to deepen and complete its significance. This it has, bequeathed unwillingly by an expedition leader chosen for his romance rather than his sense. Again the moon was extraordinarily bright, dazzling, hanging above us there like a street lamp, and I lay awake for long, contented periods under the stars, listening to the land, thinking of fate and circumstance, of history and the future, dreaming with my eyes open.

LOOKING ROUND THE BEND OF THE EARTH

When Ratcliffe reached the Cooper in 1935, it was near the end of a long drought and he crossed the dry channels 'downstream', closer to Lake Eyre. For him there was no moon that night and the endless flat bed of grey silt presented 'an awful scene, so colourless, and so utterly unfriendly as to be almost menacing'. The creek was haunted, he wrote, 'by no friendly and comprehensible ghosts, but by the spirits of broken tribes which died misunderstood'. It was his job to sift and study the sandhills. He was at first puzzled by the presence of scattered stones, big and small, whole and broken. 'It was not until I picked up a beautifully fashioned quartzite spearhead that we realized their true significance. Practically every hill we examined showed signs of blackfellows' activities.' The few Aboriginal people he encountered seemed aloof, dirty and sombre-eyed. They gave him 'rather a start when I walked into the middle of them standing there silent and almost invisible in the darkness'. Others were away down the river, attending a corroboree. He did not speak to any, but the thought of them disturbed him as his mind searched for sleep.

His uneasiness at the Cooper was also founded in his horror at the state of the land. Four years after his flying fox survey, Ratcliffe was recalled to Australia to report on the problem of soil drift. The 'dirty thirties' were nightmare years for pastoralists. Ratcliffe described soil erosion as 'a creeping cancer of the land' and inland Australia as 'nothing less than a battlefield'. He visited and investigated the arid pastoral belt of inland South Australia and south-west Queensland, where overstocking had denuded the natural vegetation of saltbush. This was in the same years that the full disaster of the American dust bowl became apparent. The parallels between the western frontiers of Australia and America again must have confronted Ratcliffe and his father. In Australia, as on the Great Plains of the United States, it was a time of extended drought – most of the stations Ratcliffe passed had failed to register their average annual rainfall in any year since 1921.

Again he travelled inquisitively, listening, observing and asking questions, seeking out and using the local networks of talk and information, so that the people were as much his subject of study as the soil, the plants and the wildlife. He described a duststorm every three days and a bad one every week – a bad one meant that you got half a kerosene tin of dust and sand out of every room. 'The air,' he said, 'was as thick as a London fog.' The storms darkened their homes as well as their lives. 'Here the folk lived indoors in a perpetual twilight, behind lace curtains and half-drawn blinds.' Hundreds of sheep might be buried alive in a bad storm, graziers went around with their hair hard and grey, their hands with 'the almost greasy feeling which a fine dust brings', the taste of dust in their mouths. Even their eyes were grey, said Ratcliffe, 'a queer, opaque look, whitening around the iris rim, like those of someone going slowly blind', with strain wrinkles around them, their mouths tight-lipped to keep out the dust as much as the flies. Farmers habitually sat by the open door of their homes gazing at the horizon. Just outside, the rain gauge had pride of place, and inside, hanging on the walls, was the favoured form of decoration in arid Australia: historic photographs of floods.

Ratcliffe visited deserted homesteads where farmers had

named their paddocks 'Purgatory', where the drift sand piled to the top of the windows, where stockyards were buried, where even river-beds disappeared under sand dunes so that you could only see the very tops of the coolibah trees poking out like little bushes. When the wind blew, sand penetrated everywhere, below the doors, in drifts against the feet. You went to sleep listening to the hiss of the blowing sand against the corrugated iron walls. 'We breathed sand, drank sand and ate sand; and when we blinked our eyeballs grated. Sand was in the butter, in the sugar, in the cake, and in the vegetables.' Dinner rituals could be bizarre: sometimes, unbelievably, they had to put their plates under the tablecloth at meals, poke about blindly with knife and fork, and put the mouthfuls away as quickly as possible before too much sand collected in the food.

Ratcliffe also saw this land – the Channel Country – animated by water, a place where rain falling hundreds of kilometres away to the north-east periodically floods down and over dry channels, bringing a spectacular pulse of life to the plains. When he returned to the Cooper the following year, 1936, he felt that it was like returning to 'the tiger's paws from which I had so recently escaped … The tiger, moreover, was no longer slumbering, for the drought had broken, and the great inland rivers had come down in flood.' 'In the end it took us three weeks to get over the wretched "creek" ', he said of the Cooper. A fresh came down and blocked him at Windorah, near where the Barcoo and Thomson rivers join to form the Cooper and where the creek flares out into its myriad channels.

Ratcliffe the scientist found that his objectivity collapsed under the weight of an overpowering fear and depression. Listen to what the 'kingdoms of dust' did to this eminently sensible, if nervous European who eventually made his home in Australia:

> … the vastness, the loneliness, and the desolation of …
> [the area] broke through my mental defences; and once
> they had cracked, it was impossible to weld them
> together again … [I became] sickeningly conscious of
> the immensity and emptiness of the land … We seemed
> to be looking round the bend of the earth … I thought
> it was just about the cruellest and most inhuman world
> that it was possible to conceive … I was uncomfortable
> and nervous now: later I was to be really scared –
> scared that something in my mind would crack, that
> the last shreds of my self-control would snap and leave
> me raving mad. … My mind was dominated by one
> idea – to get out of that ghastly country before I went
> crazy.

The solution, which, as he put it, was 'not the answer I wanted or hoped to find', was a critical appraisal of Australian inland settlement, again a whole landscape solution, striving for a social as well as natural balance:

> The essential features of white pastoral settlement [he
> wrote] – a stable home, a circumscribed area of land,

and a flock or herd maintained on this land year-in and year-out – are a heritage of life in the reliable kindly climate of Europe. In the drought-risky semi-desert Australian inland they tend to make settlement self-destructive.

Ratcliffe wrote that Australians 'had every reason to be intensely proud of their record in settling the great spaces of the inland'. 'They are only to be blamed,' he continued, 'in that they seem to have done the job too thoroughly.' At a time when 'Australia Unlimited' was still a powerful expectation, when the yeoman ideal remained politically dominant, when populating the inland was a patriotic duty, Ratcliffe had the temerity to conclude that the only thing that would preserve the country would be 'consciously to plan a decrease in the density of pastoral population of the inland'.

THE POLITICS OF NATURE

Ratcliffe's style of science reminds me of an earlier ecological vision when social, humanist dimensions were more easily, more naturally integrated. Ecologists have since incorporated sophisticated quantitative techniques and theories from the physical sciences, hoping to make ecology a 'hard science'. And so the social, human dimension has often become a factor that had to be read out, a non-natural disturbance or intrusion that lay outside the real equation. This is changing again now, the pendulum is swinging back, and Ratcliffe's practice emerges from the past as a model.

He came to Australia to study single-issue problems and he responded with holistic ecological studies and social commentaries. He came as much to study people as nature, to listen more than to teach, his concerns ranged across wildlife and ecology, he looked for whole landscape solutions, he bravely argued the reality of environmental limits, and he took seriously his duty to communicate his findings to a general public. He regarded people not only as components of the ecosystem, but also as sources of knowledge about it. Ratcliffe listened. He did not just hand down scientific knowledge from on high. He derived it from the people who lived it, as well as from his own expertise. '[E]very one of my prophesies in connection with this work has proved wrong so far', he mused about flying foxes. 'My present investigation is turning out to be 90% common sense and 10% science', he wrote. Sometimes he worried that science, as well as people, degenerated at the ends of empire.

His naturally intuitive, holistic approach led him to be reluctant about interventionist techno-fixes; he was wary of the 'silver bullet' and felt the need to address as well the enduring social and psychological problems of the landowner. His fieldwork, although it included observation in the wild, began at the homestead table and it ended there. For it was these people who would have to understand, support and enact his recommendations. So, for Ratcliffe, it was always a dialogue, always an historical as well as scientific investigation, always an active and respectful enrolment of the locals, even if he ended up disagreeing with them.

Therefore, the book that Ratcliffe ended up writing was not just a report, it was a strategy. The first half was written on his return to Britain with 'the object of lightening the darkness of the northern Scottish winters by calling up memories of antipodean warmth and sunshine'. Whilst travelling, the idea of a book had begun brewing in his mind, and his letters home were effectively his first drafts. In the archives, blue lines down the margins of his letters indicate the passages he thought suitable for publication. 'If I write my book, [he confessed] … I shall have to let fly pretty hard on this point … that the public life of the Australian is about as low a development as civilisation can afford to produce.' In May 1930, he wrote to his father: 'I have decided that I shall have a shot at writing a book about Queensland when my job is through … I think I shall wait, however, until I am safely out of the country.'

Ratcliffe did indeed wait and a few years later he submitted to London publishers Chatto and Windus an account of his adventures with the flying fox in Queensland. But while awaiting their opinion, he found himself recalled to Australia, and suddenly he was no longer 'safely out of the country'. When news of the acceptance of the manuscript arrived about 1936, he hastily read the text again and, as he put it:

> … immediately cabled that publication should be held up until I had made certain cuts and alterations. These I considered advisable, even necessary, since I had taken up a permanent position in Australia, with a certain

amount of dignity to uphold. The cuts included anything which might conceivably give offence in official circles.

Once he had completed all the necessary cuts, he found the remaining manuscript to be 'very much on the short side', so he recommended that he fill it out again with an account of his 'wanderings in the inland on the trail of drifting sand'. So the book evolved, and in doing so, the judgments of a departing visitor softened to those of resident who would have to live with the consequences of his words.

But it was actually more complex than that. The book that Ratcliffe might have written, a shorter book about 'chasing bats over a half-civilised continent', would have charged the Australian people with irresponsibility in both domestic politics and environmental management, claiming that antipodean nature had to be defended from this impoverished, transplanted society that was British Australia. The people were degenerate, lazy, small-minded and violent towards nature – the land was endangered by their lack of moral character. The book that he actually wrote surprisingly reversed the judgment. It acclaimed the people and offered a severe assessment of the land. The moral character of the people redeemed a harsh environment. Partly it was the wise diplomacy of a traveller-turned-immigrant. But it was also a consequence of the second half of his adventures as a biologist, his exposure to inland Australia.

In the 1930s there was a rapid rise in the popularity of books about the Australian inland. Australia's 'vast open spaces' were being discovered and celebrated. Remote regions had become more accessible, and there was a turning to country virtues in the wake of the devastating losses of the Great War, and the economic crash of the late 1920s. Anxiety about the defence of apparently empty territory quickened, and debates about the land were also debates about the White Australia policy, immigration and fears about the decline in population growth. One could not discuss space without also discussing race.

Ratcliffe's book was deeply radical in its trenchant criticism of the environmental impact of pastoralism and in its perception and articulation of the limits of Australian settlement. His suspicion of technology and his preference for the social solution extended to a rejection of the technological answers which boosters offered to the development of the inland. He preferred 'to fit the social and economic order to the natural one'. Such an assertion of intractable Australian environmental distinctiveness was not just a product of ecological insights, however, for it also intersected with a newly emerging environmental politics. In his book *Anxious Nation*, David Walker argues that the 1930s saw a more ready recognition of Australia as a harder, drier, browner land: 'the more Australia was perceived as a continent with its own unique flora, fauna and landscapes, the harder it was to imagine it as a continent designed for Asian settlement'. The discovery of the environmental distinctiveness of Australia undermined the assumption that the continent had 'Asian' affinities that might make it more suited to Asian than to European settlement.

Walker describes how research in the interwar years on Australian population, settlement and resource management was often presented at forums organised by the Institute of Pacific Relations, Honolulu, by speakers conscious of the need to convince Asian delegations that Australia was a geographically distinct continent, with limited population-carrying capacity. 'This need to explain Australia to an Asian audience often led, quite literally, to the creation of an Australia that was not meant to appeal to Asian nations seeking settlement opportunities abroad.'

Flying Fox and Drifting Sand was one of five books chosen in the late 1950s to be printed for the 'Cheap Books Scheme for Asia', a secret plan to combat Communism by competing with 'the flood of cheap books provided in Asia by Soviet Russia'. R.G. Casey, Minister for External Affairs and Minister responsible for the Australian Secret Intelligence Service, wrote in 1959 to the Treasurer Harold Holt of the need to identify books that would:

> … illustrate themes which seem likely to create a favourable climate for Australia among Asians. The kinds of theme which I have in mind would include the absence of racial prejudice in Australia, the idea of Australia as a waterless land unsuitable for mass settlement, Australia's past and continuing pioneering efforts – the absence of that decadence attributed to capitalist societies in communist propaganda, our progressive social reforms and the egalitarian nature of Australian society,

our [respect] request for human and spiritual rights without the extreme materialism of either Communism or American individualism, the primitive nature of our aborigines and of the New Guinea peoples, and even the beneficial aspects of colonial regimes.

At the time that he wrote this letter, Casey had identified three of the other four books to be pumped into Asia alongside *Flying Fox and Drifting Sand*, ten or more thousand copies of each of them. They were E.W. Titterton's *Atomic Energy*, Vladimir Petrov's *Empire of Fear*, and Douglas Mawson's *Home of the Blizzard*.

THE ECONOMY OF WATER

At the end of the century, I found hope by the Cooper, not despair. It was not just the good season.

Outside Windorah, near where Ratcliffe spent three frustrated weeks trapped by the ebullient flow of his dead creek, we are sitting by the water talking ecology with the locals. The Mayor of the Barcoo Shire, Bruce Scott, uses words like 'braided' and 'anastomosing' and 'ephemeral'. They don't always quite fit in his mouth and sometimes mutate in the process, but he knows their power and meaning and politics better than any lexicologist.

Pastoralists along the Cooper happily embellish their language now with these scientific terms, eagerly adopting and adapting the words of urban professionals to advocate the special attributes of their water system. One of them, full of genuine wonder, calls the channels 'anastomazing'.

This is one of the legacies of an extraordinary and effective alliance since 1995 between pastoralists, greenies and some Aboriginal people to defend Cooper's Creek from regulation for irrigation. The language superbly captures the meeting and melding of cultures. Windorah pastoralists, I found, often begin sentences with the words: 'I'm not a radical greenie, but …' Their rivers are not only unregulated but also unpolluted. 'There's no pee in our river' they say of the (frequently misspelt) Thomson.

There are the floods – or I should say, the flow. It's not a flood but a flow; it's not a river but a creek. The braided channel system. As one stockman put it, it's not like you cross the Cooper and that's it. You cross the Cooper, and then you cross it again, and then again, and then again. And the flow swells to a sea. It is the largest inland draining system in the world.

The system is at such a whole landscape scale that you simply cannot ignore it. Its rhythms are overwhelming. Debris in trees and on fencelines records the last height of flow.

I had this simplistic idea that the country got more marginal the further one went out. But the Channel Country and large swathes of central and western Queensland – particularly the mitchell grass country – defy that expectation. There is an ownership mosaic of large company holdings and smaller private landholders, and the companies are gradually winning. But many families here date themselves back to the Duracks and Costellos of the 1860s, providing a social continuity that is unusual, quite unlike large areas of western NSW where social instability and land degradation have been tragic partners. And although some of the signs of historical mismanagement that Ratcliffe noticed are still evident, there seems to have been no single devastating period of gross overstocking and long-term environmental damage such as western NSW experienced so cataclysmically in the 1880s and 90s. Many of the pastoralists here now talk of pasture management as much as stock management, of firing the grasses, of huge paddocks kept only for emergency feed, of planning for drought and accepting flood as a bonus, of going with the flow.

In 1995, four farmers from the Macquarie Valley of NSW proposed an agricultural development on the Cooper. They had all been involved in irrigation for over fifteen years and two of them also had long experience with sheep and cattle. Their proposed 'Currareva' development included the growing of cotton and wheat, followed by more intensive horticultural and viticultural activities, as well as a fish farming enterprise. Cotton production, with its chemicals and thirst for water, is far more disruptive of ecological processes than pastoralism has ever been.

The debate about irrigation on the Cooper is a revealing moment in the catchment's history and it made locals articulate their history and their pride, and to see the political as well as environmental advantages of talking 'sustainability'. In the face of corporate cotton, pastoralists mobilised in defence of their social as well as natural environment. It's a reversal of the more usual situation where a rural shire might be found advocating development and being restrained by government on behalf of an urban environmental sensibility. One of the leaders of the campaign was Bob Morrish, a local pastoralist with a background in psychology, who writes referenced academic papers on the natural rhythms of the Cooper system, and gives them titles like 'Aliens in the Ecosystem: The Strange Behaviour of Human Beings'. He acknowledges a lineage of Australian perspectives on 'the global ecocrisis' which includes Jock Marshall's *The Great Extermination* (1966), Leonard Webb's *The Environmental Boomerang* (1973), and Tim Flannery's *The Future Eaters* (1994). 'Small wonder,' writes Morrish, 'that the Australian novelist Xavier Herbert described humans as the most savage and brutal animals on this earth.' In this pastoralist's mind, the fight against irrigation is placed in an historical context of international ecopolitics and a timeless and despairing psychology of humanity.

On the ground it translates into local advocacy for the Cooper as a national resource. The link between embedded locals and an educated, travelling, urban populace therefore becomes crucial, and tourism is increasingly tolerated, not only for its economic promise, but because of the expanded electorate it offers to an outnumbered and defensive few living downstream in a fragile catchment.

Bruce says that people come here and are almost disappointed that they do not find it more barren, even in drought. They expect just red dust and tumbleweeds. I asked him what he wanted them to learn. He said he would like them to see how the country is still habitable after 100–150 years of

European settlement, that people have learned to live with the land, with the ecosystems because they have no choice. Few of the towns here are on artesian or sub-artesian water supplies; they rely on the surface water in all its unreliability. People live with that. The pulse of life that enlivens the ecosystems is what the people, too, must live off. He did not think that there should be more people out here, or that development should entail meddling with the water supply. He talked self-sufficiency and integrity of systems, the economy of Cooper water spilling over into all his politics.

As I write these words, I am reminded of Ratcliffe's letters written home from the Queensland frontier, spun out of the talk in paddocks and homesteads. As one Channel Country pastoralist and naturalist said to me, it is wrong that our species lists of various regions do not include *homo sapiens*.

THE VEINS OF THE LAND

In this extraordinarily flat land, there are few places to climb up for a view from above, few vantage points for an aerial perspective. Yet you do indeed feel like you are looking round the bend of the earth. The horizons are immense and distant yet you feel as if you might be falling over the edge of them. And the skies are stretched canvases of dramatic effects. What would it be like to be in them, to be up there, to be vertically advantaged in this awesome horizontality?

That's the stock European urge, isn't it, to want to be high up and to look down? That's seen to be imperial and dominating and controlling. And it's the urge that propels thousands of unfit people every year to ignore Aboriginal pleas and climb Uluru. If you are embedded in the land spiritually and environmentally, perhaps you don't need this view from outside and from above. Or perhaps you divine such a view intuitively. It is an intriguing mystery that Aboriginal art and map-making so effectively imagined the aerial perspective.

Sandy Kidd of Windorah gave us that view with the aid of imported technology. When I met him he seemed like he was carved out of red granite, with only his jaw moving and that barely. As he sat by a waterhole, upon newly graded earth where a deadly snake had just slithered, he looked around with pride and announced his affection for the place: 'I wouldn't call the king me uncle in this place. I couldn't catch a cold here.' Later as we awaited dinner at his home, he handed us beer cans spattered with blood from the chiller. 'The Channels, eh? I didn't know I loved them so much till they tried to bugger them up.' Sitting in the red dust or flying in the blue sky were both equally easy and natural for him. He has a big red airstrip in his backyard, and kangaroos are a hazard. He learned to fly in paddocks in Charleville and Toowoomba in 1956.

Sandy showed us a photo of his father as a child with well-dressed Aboriginal carers; his dad was delivered by an Aboriginal midwife in Cunnamulla. And he spoke earnestly of how much knowledge of the land and its rhythms, the plants and animals, came from 'the old blacks', transmuted into a common bush lore, but its source not entirely forgotten. In the air, a view the old blacks never had, this bush pilot seemed to find another meeting with their minds.

Sandy flew at about 250 feet and sometimes lower mostly over his property 'Ourdel' near Windorah. He followed one particular channel branching out from the Cooper system, the one which the irrigation development at Currareva would have drained. Banking low over the outlet, he commented upon its small beginning and then followed with his wings the extent of its influence as a web of natural irrigation channels spread out from it. From the air the hydraulics were exposed, the tapestry was revealed, the tracery – and it is the right word, so expressive of finery and fragility – was suddenly manifest.

I thought about the importance of the aerial perspective in helping us to understand the scale and integrity of the system. Satellite photos of the Channel Country (and we saw one at the Stockman's Hall of Fame) look like microscope slides of organic tissue. There is a strong connection in the outback between flying and health – John Flynn's famous Inland Mission and the Flying Doctor Service – and here the health that is exposed for scrutiny, the veins that are laid out, are ecological. The bones can be discerned, too, the geological structures of deep time. One looks down through space – *and* time, across millions of years. It is impossible not to see connections between new ecological understandings and the aerial perspective, particularly in flat landscapes, particularly in the Channel Country which is a creation of flat land and sudden water. No imperial gaze this view from above, but a dawning, embedded insight.

173

When councillors of the Barcoo Shire were considering
the consequences of the proposed 'Currareva' development, a
deputation flew to Narromine in the Macquarie Marshes to
speak with graziers about the consequences of cotton farming
in that region. The testimony was very disturbing. 'There were
quite a few people there with symptoms of chemical poisoning and spoke of their experiences', reported Bruce Scott to his
fellow councillors. The Barcoo representatives were urged not
to trust the promises of cottongrowers. They were taken for a
drive around the Marshes and everywhere they could 'really
see the effects of lack of water, huge river red gum trees hundreds of years old dead and dying, areas where river couch and
water reeds once grew all dead'.

But just as important as this on-ground survey and direct
oral testimony was the view from the air as they flew home.
Bruce concluded his report with these words on the lessons of
an aerial perspective about his own land:

> We then flew home right along Coopers Creek from
> about Nappamerrie to Tanbar via Lake Yamma Yamma.
> You can really see how little water there is in the system
> after two floods. There is hundreds of thousands of acres
> that never received a drop of water.

There is no surplus water here. The floods are the flow. The
rivers are creeks. And they do indeed, as Francis Ratcliffe discerned, 'have spirits of their own'.

les murray

THE BELLWETHER BRUSH

As the painter Sali Herman discerns
and captures the iron-lace character
of what are still called slums then
he's unaware the bright haze his brush
confers is called Billions;
he delightedly thinks Beauty, Truth,
but fashion turns its head, and starts
walking clap-clap in the footsteps,
clap-clap, of his easel,
walking in twos, as coppers used to,
till the salt of the earth accept
hot offers for their bijou homes.

delia falconer

KENNETH SLESSOR: THE INTIMACY OF THE TABLE

> *But here I am in Sydney*
> *At the age of sixty-one*
> *With the clock at a quarter to bedtime*
> *And my homework still not done.*
> — Kenneth Slessor

I WAS TWENTY WHEN I met the great poet. It seemed to me then that I would always live in a long and narrow flat in a street between two steeples, that there would always be a bright arm of the harbour glimpsed sidelong through the eye's corner as I read in trams or trains. All that year I wore a shabby cream suit with a crimson handkerchief folded at the breast and a hip flask in one pocket. This day I had a nervous quiver in the corner of my mouth, my hair was brilliantined and combed. Is it possible that I also clutched a sheaf of my own poems, in a buckram folio, marked with the date and place of their composition, in the hope that he might notice them? I admit I did.

It was late on a summer afternoon when I climbed the steps to the Journalists' Club at the back of Central Station. The bar was dark; the sun still squeezed in transverse cracks of heat through the edges of the blinds and the air was close and thick, as if it had been strained through dirty corduroy.

I saw him immediately, at a table in the furthest corner, the thin neck and browless eyes I recognised from photographs, that broad and wizzened head, the blue bow tie. There was a claret and a paper and a jug of water on the table. He wore a double-breasted suit, fastidiously buttoned. He made notes as he read the paper with a crabbed hand in a tiny notebook. From where I stood at the bar, ten feet away, I could hear the sharp, swift indentations of the pencil.

I wonder now exactly what I expected from him. I still imagined then that each writer knew himself as part of a brotherhood of authors, that the rules were sensible and clear, that one great writer would always recognise another. I had come across his famous poem for the first time in my school reader where it had been placed, miraculously, among the work of well-known, foreign poets; and I could still recite it. I knew that he had not published another poem since.

At last he put away his heavy spectacles and came up to the bar.

'Which do you think is quickest transport up to the University, the train or bus?' he asked the barman. 'I believe I'm to deliver a paper there at the English Department in an hour.'

'No you're not,' I said.

He turned; his glare was quick and blank, the appalled expression of the recognised and put-upon which to my shame I feel sometimes flash across my own face if some reader taps me on the shoulder while I am standing at a festival with my literary friends, or if I meet a student in the street. His mouth was the same grim line which I saw on the faces of my father's friends, and I also recognised something of their brittleness, which, with some fear, I considered a symptom of the office life, as if the atmosphere of heavy ashtrays, and high-backed leather chairs, had permanently pressed itself upon them.

'It's next week. You can take my word for it.' I fished the crumpled flyer from my folio with shaking hands. I could not stop talking. 'It's true. I study there. Believe me, if there was a change of date I'd know about it.'

He nodded as he read, then shook my hand and thanked me. His palm was surprisingly bony, for he was not a small man. He had the formal kindness I was later to associate with men who spent long periods of time alone, the outback reserve of country gentlemen or mining engineers. 'I've been dying to read your next collection,' I said.

'Not dying, I hope.' His eyes had lost a little of their flint. 'I'm sure there are better things to die for.'

We moved to the table he had just abandoned. 'Do you drink claret?' I nodded although I did not. 'Good,' he said, as he waved the barman over. 'Rituals are the great comfort of growing older. It is important to remember that eating and drinking are also a kind of life. I knew a man once, a barrister, whose great pleasure in life was to go to the Lawyers' Club in Bridge Street – do you know it? – they served up English boarding school food, quite dreadful preparations, at tuck shop prices: tapioca, sago, trifle with the hint of the stale and con-fiscated cake about it. The rest of us would amuse ourselves by making up new names for the dishes: Matron's Surprise, willow sausage, flannel soup. My friend was a rather wealthy man, but I have never seen him happier than when he ate their thrippeny tart with custard.'

I could only nod, faced with the scrupulous mechanics of his conversation. The club began to fill. Occasionally, one of the men, with the lines of his hat still on his forehead would loom and greet him loudly. He responded quietly and intro-duced me to them as his 'friend'. Yet I could sense his eyes move across the backs lined up at the bar and felt he would soon dismiss me, before I could show him my poems about flying foxes and Moreton Bay figs, or ask him why he did not write.

He asked me where young people 'went' these days. I said I did not know; that I was fairly solitary 'by choice' because I was 'too busy writing', that I did go to the 'usual' Greek cafeterias in Castlereagh Street; and that I went sometimes with my friend Robert who was a student politician to the branch meetings to which he was so frequently invited. He had no particular political calling, but had calculated that by this means we could save ourselves the price of around three meals a week. He had chosen the Liberal Country Party because the girls tended to be richer and the catering of a higher standard. The disadvantage was that we had often to travel up and down the north shore train line. We travelled to Willoughby only if the necessity was very great, for this required a bus, and the hostess at this particular branch served without fail mayonnaise on a lettuce leaf balanced precariously on a piece of toast.

He had a charming way of laughing. He chuckled gently with his hands placed across his belly, bending back slightly, as if he took pleasure in gauging its vibrations.

I siezed my chance. I told him where I lived, next to the deaf hospital in a pink federation villa which had been divided into bedsits; about the bathroom with its view of the railway tracks and the long ferny garden, the toilet pressed at an ungainly angle in the corner, the cantankerous water heater which I lit before each shower. I had been talked into minding a friend's axolotl which hung suspended in its green tank on the washstand and regarded my ablutions with the single lugubrious eye which remained in its possession.

'Is there a Salvation Army trombonist?' he asked. 'And an old lady with two sycophantic pomeranians and an addiction to epsom salts?'

There were no musicians, I said, but there was a thin American cartoonist who went out each Saturday evening and who, if he returned alone, played Mario Lanza on the gramophone and sang until the early morning. And once, I said, disturbed by his music which drifted unimpeded into my always-open windows, I had looked out of the bathroom at the grounds behind the deaf hospital and observed in the moonlight a game of naked rugby played in perfect silence.

The claret bottle was empty. 'Let's go to Holderigger's,' he said.

The evening was diffuse and golden. Above us, the golfer on top of Sharpie's Golf House began, endlessly, to guide his bouncing neon chip shot along its illuminated path towards the nineteenth hole.

At last, off a lane at the centre of the city, we entered a chilly portico of sandstone and passed through a set of double doors into a restaurant. I could smell the starch of the tablecloths, the sweet and desiccated scent of breadsticks. The mirrors were deep and edged with brass, the walls panelled with some dark unshining wood which still held the thrill of polish. The maître d' greeted him by name.

'And how is Madame Holderigger?' he asked the waiter.

'She's very well, Sir. Her grandson graduated this afternoon, in engineering, so she won't be coming in this evening.'

'That's splendid news. Please convey my congratulations.'

He sat, without glancing backward, in the heavy armchair as the waiter pushed it in and draped the napkin across his lap. I hesitated when the waiter gestured; I perched on the chair's edge, then readjusted it myself.

'I have known Madame Holderigger,' he said, when the waiter left us, 'for almost forty years. She is a Swiss, originally. She must be nearly ninety. You will no doubt have seen her at some event or other. She wears her hair scraped up into a tiny lacquered topknot like a cocktail onion. Many years ago she used to run some private clubs – when I was a young journalist she still had a reputation for *sly-grogging*.'

Although I smiled I had begun to panic. I had imagined, when he first suggested it, that Holderigger's was another bar. I realised now that I had not enough money for this sober restaurant. I began to say that I should be on my way at once, that I was not particularly hungry.

If I had another appointment, he said, he understood, but asked if he might show me something first. He reached into the inside pocket of his jacket, opened a leather bill-fold on the table, and produced a cheque for five pounds. It was a royalty, he said, for his last collection, published twenty years before. One should regard writing simply as a pleasant hobby, he said. In this way, any reward would come as a surprise, rather than one's due. It was his great pleasure, when those cheques turned up, to buy dinner for his friends.

Our meal arrived which he had 'taken the liberty' to order. It was the first time that I had tasted oysters on the half-shell, or seen a salad tossed at the table or a fillet steak girdled tightly by a piece of bacon. We drank a bottle of red wine. I remember that he spoke – as he forked and cut methodically with his dry white hands – of the board of the *Bulletin* and its effect on various journalists unknown to me, which I could only, dumbly, nod at; of other restaurants where I had not yet been; of his cadet days covering pet shows and sewing fairs and go-kart races where young boys with cunning faces lashed fox terriers like Mawson's huskies.

As the food came he pointed out the rituals of the service, the way the waiters wheeled out another table and placed it by our own, the way they plated out the vegetables from a serving platter. In this way the labour of the kitchen remained invisible but the hospitality of the cook was performed before us, recreating what he referred to as the 'intimacy of the table'. He also made me observe the salmon-coloured tablecloths and napkins which created, with the brass and wood, the atmosphere of a cruising liner. The pale green menus which the waiters carried worked like a contrasting thread which relieved and lifted up the orange, he said, wound by their constant movements through the room.

Towards the end of the meal he ordered another bottle of the claret. My eyes were vague and heavy, but he sat upright, a posture I have come to think of since as the mark of a truly dedicated drinker, movement conserved, the body held in a state of relaxed anticipation. He seemed, if anything, to have become more pale and grave.

I do recall that a younger waiter about my own age arrived and dug clumsily with his corkscrew at the cork. The poet flinched and snatched the bottle from his hands. He opened it himself with a single turn and twist and poured out two full glasses.

At last he asked me who I liked to 'read'. I had been read-ing the minor poets for the last few months, I said, but remained rather fond of Larkin. I found his use of para-rhyme quite daring. I stopped. There was the hint of a smile on his thin lips. Yet I sensed the chill edge of some distilled, exquisite anger.

Poetry should be the least interesting of topics to a young man my age, he said. Did I find myself at present in a domes-tic situation?

I looked down, and blushed. No, I said, at last. Of course, I added quickly, there had been 'encounters'. I hoped the term was vague enough. He gestured for the bill.

The laneway was still and damp. He hunched over a cig-arette and I noticed that he swayed a little as he lit it. I thought I could smell the Tank Stream which ran for blocks beneath our feet.

In the end, he said at last, as if he spoke to no-one, he rec-ommended women highly. Women, with their tight little jackets and impossible perfumes, he continued, had always infuriated him more than they had pleased him. But they were indispensable for poets.

He turned and looked at me intently. 'They understand faith, you see.'

I was not sure if I should laugh.

He straightened and seemed suddenly quite sober. He began to walk, stiffly, ahead of me, in the direction of the Cross. Seriousness was the affliction of old men, he said. Here was a limerick I might enjoy:

There was once a girl, called Priscilla
Whose pubes were of perfect chinchilla
each day she would trim
The hairs of her quim
And use them each night as a pill-ah.

He smiled tightly. His was a rather pedestrian para-rhyme, he feared, compared with Larkin's.

I followed because he seemed to like my company, or at least he did not mind it. He showed me the boarding house where Virgil the hunch-backed artist had invited pretty girls and sketched them for *Smith's Weekly*. And once he took me through a breach in a wall behind a block of flats where there was a mossy grotto, its steps and niches carved into the cliff. He said it was all that remained of one of the colony's first gardens and the optimism of that time.

His building was a white mansion, divided into quarters. The carpets of the vestibule were grey. I had glimpsed a small chandelier behind one window. There were dwarf maples in the garden. Inside, I exclaimed at the view. The harbour, lit by the moon, filled the window of the lounge room. The water had the febrile glow of cine-film, I added. He appeared with two glasses from the kitchen and searched a drawer for coasters. He said he was glad I liked it.

The flat was dustless. I could see a music room with books of libretto piled up on the floor, his study beyond it which also faced towards the harbour. I noticed gradually the smell of thinning carpet and dark suits.

He poured two whiskies and added water with a silver teaspoon from a jug. No ice, he said, not ever. And one teaspoon only. The water released the flavour of the Scotch. He had also brought out a platter of stilton and some water crackers. 'Some of life's small compensations.' He placed them in front of the sofa where I sat. He settled in his armchair.

I had placed my folio on the floor and it sat between us. His eyes closed each time he sipped the Scotch.

'When I was a cadet journalist, about your age,' he began quite suddenly, 'I was approached to write a small pamphlet on Australian vineyards. In Victoria I discovered that I despised everything about the countryside – the low skies filled with imperturbable grey clouds, the mournful cattle, the tattered yellow paddocks – but the wines were pleasantly surprising. On my last day there I met a German who made ice wines. The wine he brought out for me was miraculous; clear and sharp, and infinitely sad, as if cursed with an awareness of its own chill depths.

'He took three more bottles from the cellar and we walked across the yard towards his house. I had come to expect a cautious wife, a prolific flock of children, but the house was empty and quite bare, with the exception of a piano and a clock. There was a variety of corks lined up along the piano lid and there were grafted grape vines, their roots bound up in handkerchiefs, between us on the table.

'Each winter, he told me, he waited for the perfect temperature to pick his grapes. For a fortnight he would set thermometers among the vines and sit a vigil, singing songs to the mice to keep himself awake. The grapes had to be picked, with the ice still on them, at precisely minus four degrees. By the second bottle he had become quite sentimental, and with the third he began to stop every few minutes and look nervously about the room. I remember that he said he thought he was probably the greatest aristrocrat upon this earth. For he could not bear, even for a second, the thought of any uncomplicated pleasure.'

A distant foghorn sounded on the harbour.

'I have thought of him quite often since.'

I went to speak again but he seemed to have withdrawn himself from the room and into his armchair by some elusive alteration of his posture. He did not offer me another whiskey. When I stood he jumped up to see me out.

At the door he shook my hand and said he hoped that we would meet again although I knew he did not mean it. He brushed aside my thanks for dinner. He said he hoped I had not found it boring. I said sincerely I had not.

'A young man who wanted to be a poet once asked for my advice,' he said. 'I told him. Invest in fine stationery. Be open to all social occasions. Always be shaved by a barber.'

I expected him to smile but his face appeared remote and blank again and he closed the door behind me.

Random laughter drifted from the high white cupolas of the Del Ray apartments next door. The smell of gardenias mingled with the weed and mussels of the sea wall. I flattered myself, as I stood for a moment between the dwarf maples, that he stood at the darkened window, watching. Then I began to walk towards my narrow rooms.

AUTHOR'S NOTE

The headquote is the last stanza of Kenneth Slessor's last published poem which begins 'I wish I were at Orange ...', written for class 5A at Orange in April 1962. It appears in Geoffrey Dutton's *Kenneth Slessor: A Biography* (Melbourne: Penguin, 1991), p. 11.

During my undergraduate years at Sydney University in the 1980s I was friends with the young men who belonged to the Poetry Society. It was only a decade and a half later, when I discovered Slessor myself, that I realised how much they had modelled themselves upon him: in their romantic poems about the harbour and the inner-city, certain ideals of masculine behaviour, and their dress (including, in one instance, a red bow tie). This story, a work of fiction, is intended not as an accurate portrait of Slessor, but as an homage to his shadow which still haunts the Sydney streets.

peter goldsworthy

HAL PORTER: THE WATCHER WITH A CAST-IRON ALIBI

1.

IN HAL PORTER'S 1965 STORY, *Young Woman in a Wimple*, the narrator is sitting in a train compartment reading a smuggled-in copy of Vladimir Nabokov's banned novel *Lolita* 'which, in its remade brown paper jacket, looked exactly like a banned book – probably *Lolita*'.

A nice joke, but there's surely a thesis or three to be written about the significance of the books that fiction writers have their characters read. Porter's self-described 'Early Incandescent' prose-style (no less incandescent later in his life) resembles the style of few other writers as much as Nabokov's.

Whole chunks of their autobiographies, in particular, seem stylistically interchangeable. Porter's *The Watcher on the Cast-Iron Balcony* was published before Nabokov's *Speak, Memory* but the specifications are identical: intensely visual, photographically fine-detailed, stylistically dandified, and prone to feats of reverie. As well, both are inclined to epigrammatic sentences – 'I am all too aware that although one cannot become perfect even in a hundred years, one can be corrupted in an hour', 'Having no past the young are condemned to repeat everyone else's', 'Blood is thicker than water, but not than indifference'.

All Porter's work, this time.

The pervasive mood of both memoirs is nostalgia for a lost past.

Curious that such similar literary sensibilities should be thrown up by such different cultural backgrounds: the one urban-Russian, patrician, cultivated, multilingual, hugely travelled, exiled; the other country-Australian, lower middle-class, local. Hal Porter hadn't travelled more than a hundred miles from Melbourne until well into adulthood, but was perhaps emotionally exiled from the past by the death of his mother.

The temper of both narrative minds is conservative in the extreme, not surprising in such intense memoirists – memoir is an act of conservation, if nothing else. As young writers both are precociously knowing, and know that they are knowing. Both are in love with the sounds of their own voices – and why not? So are we, their readers.

At fifteen … I have developed an outrageous taste,
eclectic to eccentricity, in authors: Dickens, Olive
Schreiner, Tchekhov, Katherine Mansfield, Maupassant,
Paul Fort, Ibanez, Tolstoi, Gabriele D. Annunzio, Hardy
and Barrie. I am so fascinated by Remy de Gourmont
that I translate into an exotic English everything of his I
can lay my hands on.

From *Speak, Memory*, surely – until the next lines give the
game to Porter:

All this boils down to nothing except that an upstart
and word-obsessed adolescent is self-educating himself
towards an aim, not to this day accomplished, of stating
as incandescently as possible verities not yet fully
realised.

The cagey Nabokov would never make such a humble, or even
faux-humble, admission.

Porter, at least in the first book of autobiography, is also
more sexually open:

It is inevitable, it advances autobiography minutely and
effortlessly, to come to another and yet another first
experience. Even with memory patching what reality
must have breached, it is certain that my cocoon is
wearing, here and there, thin enough to permit intrusion
on a good boy. These intrusions never really more than

brush my goodness, though they tear the sheath surrounding it. They do nothing for innocence, but have
never possessed innocence.

This in the context of the stirring of an adolescent homosexual affair, the frank details of which created some furore when
Watcher was first published. Even here, though, when his
incandescence is at its most white-hot ('I learn from him that
sex is not a game but something more dangerously exhilarat-
ing, more deadly, more victimising, a disease of the feelings, an
itch, a rage, a mania') his preferred self-image is that of the
hunted rather than the hunter – a watcher with a cast-iron
alibi.

He liked to propose a division between himself as Person
and Writer. The Writer, he claimed, doesn't care for anyone –
including its own Person. In fact, the Writer Porter later
became much more opaque, and self-deceiving about the
Porter Person – more in the style of the Nabokov whose various sexual affairs were hidden under an infinite number of
public denials and fictional onion-skins during his life. 'I'm not
homosexual. Not heterosexual. Not bi-sexual. Not impotent.
No – anti-sexual' Porter wrote in a letter to Allan Marshall
quoted in Mary Lord's biography.

Nabokov felt he was born with a naturally visual imagination – even numbers had associated colours – and Porter
wanted to be an artist for a time. For both the page is something of a canvas, a visual field teeming with all the nouns and
adjectives of colour and shape and movement and style. Both

spent much time with mothers who were focal points of colour; jewellery, clothes and boudoir furnishings seem to have fed both visual imaginations.

But let's set VN aside and concentrate on Porter's separate vision. In the September 1964 issue of *Australian Letters*, in a piece called Hal Porter's Australia, he describes the towns of South Gippsland in both pencil sketches and prose. (This was to be the nucleus of his later book, *Bairnsdale: Portrait of an Australian Country Town.*)

Human figures are largely missing from his finely-detailed drawings of houses and streets, farmyards, chookyards, banks and churches. Of the local inhabitants, he writes in conclusion: 'Details occupy them because their minds are as wide as their streets and as broad as the pastures ringing them. They leave the broader outlook and the destructive abstractions to narrower minds.'

The three volumes of Porter's autobiography – generally regarded as his finest work – move from being occupied with details (*Watcher* and *The Paper Chase*) to more than a few destructive abstractions in the last volume (*The Extra*):

> Foreigners are only truly entertaining in their natural habitat, and preferably in national costume making horrible local delicacies or hideous local knick-knacks, and giving picturesque imitations of themselves …
> The dishes of poverty are sidling into Australian menus, and the customs and habits of migrant riff-raff (escapees from their own culture, discontented,

go-getting, venal, often criminal, and very often near-moronic).

But even here, in a book which is largely literary gossip and sociopolitical misanthropy, the writing is incandescent. The pen-portraits of other writers range from the venomous (Norman Mailer) to the ambivalent (Katharine Susannah Prichard) to the affectionate (Kenneth Slessor). The pages on Slessor – the dedicatee of *Watcher* – are unforgettable. I'd love to quote them in full, I love re-reading them; here is a mere taster, the first time at a public reading that Porter lays eyes on his literary hero and future friend:

> This is he. Standing at the lectern is a – how to write it?
> – marmalade cat. That, truly, is your first impression.
> Not tall at all, your highwayman. Solid as a pineapple,
> more male than masculine, gestureless, pink-full-faced,
> with short, slicked down gingery hair, pale eyes. The
> dandy touch alone tallies with prevision. The marmalade
> cat's well-licked, sleek, diligently immaculate, fastidious-
> ness made flesh in raiment. Always easy to spring when
> a man's clothes are chosen by a woman. There's none of
> that women's magazine colour-chart taste here. He
> wears, at it were, his own inevitable fur.

Line for line, perhaps Les Murray is the only Australian writer who can compare with Porter for natural gifts, who can pour words over a page so creamily – who, in his discipline of poetry, stands out as the same kind of ring-in, or maverick from a different tradition, as Porter does in prose. Porter also wrote poetry, and Murray once told me he regarded Porter as 'the finest Rococo poet since Slessor'. Slessor, himself, wrote in a review of Porter's poetry collection *The Hexagon*:

> severely cerebral, defiantly experimental – at times the effect becomes too cryptic or too private, but the technical brilliance never falters.

Porter's autobiographies are jammed with technical brilliance, but perhaps when the incandescence fades, it is the stories that remain glowing in our minds like the after-image of a tungsten filament; stories that are usually built around one character, or a brief character-changing trajectory. The story of the prostitute Audrey in *The Paper Chase*, of the Headmaster of Prince Alfred College in Adelaide and the loss of his son in the war, of the Chinese student (also mildly fictionalised in the short story *Say to me Ronald!*), of Slessor and his wife, of Porter's impulsive marriage to Olivia (the Ardath Girl whose face adorned every second billboard at the time) after a week in a hotel bed are all acutely rendered.

Interestingly, if it's the stories that give spine to the autobiographies, it's the autobiographical content that gives spine to his officially designated short stories.

'Another restricting factor,' Porter wrote in an interview, 'is lack of imagination: pure fiction and flights of fancy are utterly beyond me.' After a list of his short stories – most of them, it seems – that he claims to have 'filched, holus-bolus, with the insolence of a shoplifter, straight out of "life"' he continues:

> Here and there, some unwriterlike delicacy stirred me to alter a name. The delicacy was demi-delicate – Miss Brockelbank to Miss Brockel, Miss Rodger to Miss Rodda, Mr Bets to Mr Steb! More often (Lack of Imagination leads to Lack of Fear) I have used actual names: Ronald Wee Soo Wat, La, Bruno Redmond-Jones, Big Bogga, Uncle Foss, Aunt Rosa Bona, Uncle Martini-Henry … One can't make up names like that. People grow into their names; it's a reckless writer who doesn't, in search of a moniker for his created monster, riffle through old dictionaries, haunt cemeteries, read bound copies of bygone newspapers until the only name possible turns up. Characters in books have no time to grow into their names.

Most of the stories, then, are autobiographical fragments – chapters that got away, or didn't make it onto the page in time for the larger canvas. As with the autobiographies proper, loss of innocence is a recurrent theme – never better than in the wonderful *First Love. Francis Silver* is another finely wrought tale of of an illusory, idealised past – but in the end, Porter can't help saying too much. The rediscovered, disappointing Francis just won't stop lithping, well after the point has been made, and made again, and the story is ruined by overkill. Is

THE WATCHER WITH A CAST-IRON ALIBI

ruined an overstatement? Getting to the ruins of a Porter story is always a fabulous trip, but in this case – to risk a little psychobabble of the type that he would have hated – his suppressed homosexual self-loathing prevents him from knowing when to stop.

Reading these stories again, I begin to think I should always start a Porter story a few pages in, or finish a page or two short of the end. If *Francis Silver* is an example of the latter, *Mr Butterfry*, one of the stories set in Japan, which builds to a driven, ferocious conclusion, is one of the former: a story that would lose little by losing a few of its early paragraphs. But too much excess – to coin a tautology – might be a small price to pay for the just-enough-excess which is Porter's normal metier. And even when the stories fail on some level as well-rounded, coherent tales, the prose is thrilling to read.

A more curious problem becomes apparent in another story, *Vulgar's the Word*.

In this piece, written in the third person, Porter sounds, oddly, almost exactly like the Patrick White he so loathed. At a blind prose-tasting *Vulgar's the Word* would almost certainly be attributed to White, both because of the prose (its style magisterial, its humour slightly pompous, its cadences deliberately dislocated, often by sentences beginning with prepositions) and because of the milieu (a bitchy caricature of lower middle-class suburbia peopled mostly by gossipy, toothless women.)

She was a Corset Advisor in a country town emporium. Since women are the only ones who understand the coarseness and savagery of women she called herself a meat-packer.

'I remember now' said Mrs Fender, handing a streaming glass. 'Jew say squash or lemon, love? Reelly, the mind is going what with this and that and the other, and getting Gran off ther premises for a day.'

'Embuggerance,' said Rube, domestically wiping the tumbler-bottom with a pink handkerchief before putting the tumbler on the arm of the Genoa velvet settee, and lighting a king-size filter-tip.

Unconscious imitation? White's highly mannered style is highly infectious; when Porter abandons the first-person, or the third-person written through one character's narrative eyes – the eyes of the Watcher – he seems to leave himself behind, or slow himself down too much; he loses all his adjectival and list-making energy, and the result (at least in this case) is pure Sarsaparilla.

Porter loathed White, and would have hated this suggestion (White loathed Porter in return – among numerous references in his letters he labels Porter 'a sac of green pus throbbing with jealousy').

Of course, a certain misanthropic eye is required in writers. Without it, how would Porter have arrived at this:

When she died she astounded us by the way she had willed her treasures. I, for one, received a number of things about which I don't recall ever expressing a desire. I inherited each thing I had silently coveted. The Will implied a cruel perception: None of you thought I knew what you were after.

He could write equally well when his pen was driven by generosity, not jaundice; the pages devoted to his Japanese housegirl, Ikuso, at the end of *The Paper Chase* are among the best things he has written: 'It cannot be that I know all about her for I know nothing but good'. And again: 'One does not strike angels without burning one's hands'.

But at some level his morality is primarily aesthetic: Japanese prostitution is preferable to Filipino, for instance, on aesthetic grounds.

THE NOVELS

I've left this difficult problem till last. If his best work – the autobiographies, and the best of the stories – is dependent on the overt presence of himself, on *his* narrative eye, his first-person Watcher, then is his (relative) absence part of the reason for the (relative) failure of the novels?

Narrative is not usually Porter's strong-suit, and perhaps the most interesting aspect of the longer 'fictions' is the parallels they offer to the autobiographies. Why, then, should they not be as successful as the stories – they are just as brimful of fascinating descriptive and autobiographical material? Because the clutter gets in the way of the big picture? Our lives are a clutter of stories and perceptions; autobiography is the story of that clutter, an attempt to make sense of it, yes, but always only in part, and always also a celebration of the clutter itself.

Novels, also, are in part a celebration of human clutter and idiosyncrasy – but Porter's imagination is not ultimately interested in the big picture the novel can also reveal; his interest, like the Devil (and like the inhabitants of Bairnsdale) is in the detail.

Perhaps his escape from the contradictions in his own life, from the solidity of some overarching narrative or understanding of himself, was also in the detail.

...is, for me
...stantly between
...tation.

n is Dead

C.
5.

and visits a prostitute who gives him
rest when rest is all he needs. All the
time his thoughts are of Tamar, the girl
from his village whom he wants to marry
before her illegitimate child, not his, is
born. Morning comes, the eel is dead,
and so, alas, are his hopes.

Despite a deadly seriousness which
causes a dangerous teetering towards
sentimentality and despite the conscious
difficulties of style, West's novel is a
... achievement. He has tried to see
...and as it is today, and through the
...nger the promised land, someone
...hom there is no promised land.
...all, there is sympathy between
...d his characters, a somewhat
...nable thing these days when
...elists disgustedly hold their
...up with tongs for our bemused

...cy, who has taken several
... original glances at Dublin
...as turned her eyes from
...city towards the well-
...und of the English home
...ero, if such he be, is
...e, a noted art-dealer,
...ho thanks God he is
... has "great faith in
... is of his infatuation
..., remarkably silly;
...he requires nothing
...learer recollection
...e young.

...ck, bright and
...omically and
...e which keeps
...oving at pace.
...r from the
...unty types.
...of varnish

...Tracy's
...hen she

...of frozen darkn...
loss, absence, nothing. Wal...
the wind
Our Lord speaks to a crowd of ...
faces.

no face that is not mine, while fi...
ing through
gaps, honeycombs of memory yo...
seem
but the faint ghost of a remembered
dream.
Unveiled by pain, I bleed. My wound
is you.

Lost in the well of space, my spirit
hears
"Lucis creator optime . . ." The choir
entreats God, out of tune. I join my
voice
to theirs. Nightfall's immense. I taste
my tears.
I reap the harvest of my own desire.
No heart escapes the torment of its
choice.

WALTER LEHMANN

Abelard to Eloisa

Far above memory's landscape let the
fears
unlatched from thundering valleys of
your mind
carry their lightning. Stare the sun up.
Find
kinetic heat to scorch your mist of
tears.

All that your vision limned by night
appears
loose in dismembering air: think yourself blind.
Louder than death in headlines the
unkind
elements hawk my passion: stop your
ears.

Deny me now. Be Doubting Thomas.
Thrust
into my side the finger of your grief.
Tell me I am an apparition frayed
out of the tattered winding-sheet of
lust.
Recall no ghost of love. Let no belief
summon me, fleshed and bleeding,
from the shade.

WALTER LEHMANN

cassandra pybus

SING MEMORY: A REVERIE FOR GWEN HARWOOD

A TODDLER IS PADDLING in the shallows while ripples of sparkling water radiate from her unsteady feet into a bay that is calm as a mill pond. Her sunbonnet is askew and the right leg of her nappy has slipped below the floral sundress. She holds a small plastic bucket in one chubby hand. In the distance, at the end of a wide sweep of sand, is a small promontory with a cluster of gum trees, and a long narrow jetty. If I examine the photo with a magnifying glass I can make out the carbide works through the trees, its perpetual white plume of ash billowing into the cloudless sky.

The untidy child is me, playing on the beach below my grandparents' house at Snug, more than fifty years ago. It is my earliest personal photograph. In the first decade of my life I spent my January holidays at Snug, a small village tucked behind a beautiful, sheltered cove of North West Bay, about thirty kilometres south of Hobart. The white plume from the carbide works and the fine film of ash which settled everywhere, remain one of my enduring childhood memories. My grandfather and my Uncle Ken were employed at the carbide works, as was nearly every man in Snug. In the early morning I would watch them all walk along the beach, then over the little wooden walkway that the Electrolytic Carbide Company had constructed across the rivulet and up through the trees to the works.

This exquisite sun-drenched spot was a very different world from the place where I was born and lived for the other months of the year, halfway up Mount Wellington, nestled among a dripping forest dominated by giant manferns, where tendrils of water seeped from every crevice in the mossy rockface and decaying leaf-litter was soft and spongy underfoot. Even in summer my home on the mountain was a dank, magical, musty place and for most of the winter it was covered in a dusting of snow. I loved it there, yet my strongest memory of that place is an intense ache in my toes as I struggled to the school-bus stop along a mile of winding mountain road glistening with black ice.

The village of Fern Tree had few services, but it was where young couples could afford to buy after the Second World

War. My young father, returning from wartime service in the Navy to find himself with a wife and son he barely knew, had bought an old house with heart-stopping views over a succession of fiords and inlets to the southern ocean. So too had Bill Harwood, who had just accepted a position in the English Department at the University of Tasmania and moved from Brisbane with his new wife. With small children much the same age, it was inevitable that my mother Betty and Gwen Harwood would encounter each other pushing their prams along the pipeline or buying provisions in the village store and strike up a friendship. They were part of a social circle of young couples who attended the monthly square-dance in the community hall and took turns to host devil-may-care parties, awash with hugely alcoholic punch, which lasted until dawn. As their menfolk spent long hours away at work in Hobart, Fern Tree by day was a world of young women like Betty and Gwen – transplanted in a strange and demanding environment away from their families – who struggled with the experience of mothering for which they felt entirely unprepared. Years later Gwen was to immortalise those early days of motherhood in her poem, 'An Impromptu for Ann Jennings':

> Sing memory, sing those seasons in the freezing
> suburb of Fern Tree, a rock shaded place
> with fern trees, gullies, snowfalls and eye-pleasing
> prospects from paths along the mountain-face.

Nursing our babies by huge fires of wattle,
or pushing them in prams when it was fine,
exchanging views on a diet, or Aristotle,
discussing Dr Spock or Wittgenstein,

cleaning up infants and the floors they muddied,
bandaging, making ends and tempers meet –
sometimes I'd mind your children while you studied,
or you'd take mine when I felt near defeat;

Together these young women ran fetes and cake stalls to raise
the funds to build a preschool to relieve them for a few hours
a day from the constant demands of children. At the Fern Tree
kindergarten I was taught my first lessons in 'being a good girl',
although much of the time I was locked in the storeroom for
my disobedience.

I still had not learned to be a good girl by the time I was
eleven and my father took me to live on the mainland. For a
few years I grieved for the vistas of mountain, sea and sky, then
I forgot about Tasmania. When memory stirred me again it was
so powerful that I could not resist its pull. In 1985 I came back
to live in Snug.

I bought the house of my Uncle Ken at Lower Snug,
across the bay from my grandfather's house, alongside the old
carriage road which ran down to the convict station at Oyster
Cove in the D'Entrecasteaux Channel. I remembered the old
station site as a place where my cousins and I used to rough-
and-tumble on the salt marsh at low tide when our parents

visited the ancient great-aunts. They lived almost next-door in a house their grandfather Henry Harrison Pybus had built only a few years before the last tribal people of Tasmania were removed from their place of exile on Flinders Island to become his pitiful neighbours in the abandoned station. When the remaining Aboriginal people had dwindled to less than a dozen, Henry Harrison offered to take care of them on his own property to keep them from harm. His modest price was too high for the government to pay, and his neighbours continued in their deplorable conditions until only one old woman, Trugernanna, survived. Lalla Rooke, as the people of Hobart liked to name her, was taken to live in town and the station was closed for ever.

That item of history did not come from my childhood memories. I had to go to the Tasmanian archives to find it. When my cousins and I went fossicking among the ruins for broken clay pipes and bits of pottery, no-one had bothered to explain that Trugernanna and her relatives had once lived there, next-door to our own family. Nor did anyone explain that the original Pybus free land grant – two and a half thousand acres – originally belonged to Trugernanna's people. It was not done to talk about such things.

I did know that my mother's old friend Gwen Harwood lived at Oyster Cove. She had been something of a heroine of mine ever since I heard about her audacious acrostic poem 'Abelard to Eloisa' in which the first letters of each line had spelt out the words 'fuck all editors'. Re-reading her *Selected Poems* in my new home, I was especially drawn to her Oyster

Cove poems in which she celebrated the extraordinary beauty of the channel country as Arcady, yet she sees it as also cold and cruel, haunted by its forlorn ghosts.

> Dreams drip to stone. Barracks and salt marsh blaze
> opal beneath a crackling blaze of frost.
> Boot-black, in graceless Christian rags, a lost
> race breathes out cold …
>   The long night's past
> and the long day begins. God's creatures, made
> woodcutters' whores, sick drunks, watch the sun prise
> their life apart: flesh, memory, a language all
> split open, featureless, to feed the wild
> hunger of history.

Since it seemed to me that if I were to continue to live in Tasmania I would have to come to terms with the terrible stories of dispossession and genocide that were embedded in the deceptively benign landscape I had re-embraced, I began fossicking in the Tasmanian archives for the evidence of my family's complicity. I wrote to Gwen about Oyster Cove and I received a thoroughly delightful letter in which she told me how she had liked to hunt for shards of history among the crumbling foundations of the old station and how she always felt the deep melancholy of that exquisite place. She included a recent poem she had written on the death of her dearest friend, the painter Edwin Tanner, 'Sunset at Oyster Cove'.

> … I fear those dreams
> when those I loved, now dead,
>   are speaking to those who died
>   in earlier times; they did not meet on earth
>   but smile and know. They bid me;
>   restore, repair, remember.
>   Be with me here as you were in pain but smiling,
>   here where the dying race
>   posed stiffly as grim dolls
>   for their last likeness, history closing round them.

It was the beginning of a very special friendship for me. Gwen Harwood, I was to learn, had a genius for letter writing as she did for friendship. As she and her husband had just left Oyster Cove to move to Hobart, I met her for lunch near the state library and was surprised to encounter a diminutive woman with a girlish face and beatific smile. I expected someone more imposing, I suppose, and more serious, since she had recently recovered from a radical mastectomy. Gwen told me people were often surprised when they met her. Hal Porter, who became another mutual friend of my parents and hers, had been hugely relieved to find she was 'just a little woman'. Having read some of her poetry he expected her to be 'a bead-hung vampire'. Over lunch she spoke about Edwin Tanner and about her memories of the old station at Oyster Cove, while I told her about the research I had begun into the dispossession of the original Tasmanians. She insisted that I should write a book. Although I had a bit of a name as a literary critic, I'd never written a book before nor even dreamed of doing such a thing. With characteristic generosity she waved aside any protest of inadequacy and offered to write a recommendation to the Tasmanian arts funding body to assist me. Gwen Harwood set me on the path to being a writer with my book *Community of Thieves* and she managed to be present in every one of my literary projects until her death from cancer six years ago.

When I told her that for my next project I would write a book about the infamous Orr case she looked suddenly solemn and her eyes lost their twinkle. I had not realised that this was a source of considerable anguish for her. She talked angrily about 'the mongrels' – not a term I had heard her use before – who had destroyed her dear friend Edwin Tanner. I had not known that Tanner had been one of Orr's accusers, along with Suzanne Kemp, or that he had been driven out of the state (and perhaps driven out of his mind) by the persecution of those who supported Orr. Gwen gave me permission to consult the letters between herself and Tanner in the Fryer library in Brisbane. What a boon that turned out to be. Apart from the vivid behind-the-scenes talk about the Orr case, the letters were simply marvellous. Even in a blind fury about Orr and his supporters, Gwen was deliciously funny. In despair that anyone was going to believe the story of Tanner and Kemp, she had proposed that her next acrostic sonnet would read SYD ORR IS GUILTY. She was furious when the university finally agreed to give £16,000 compensation to 'that ratbag' and she blamed James McAuley for it. 'This business has knocked the stuffing right out of us,' she wrote Tanner, 'we will probably be found gibbering in the corner reading Noddy books and passing each other £16,000 in play money.'

Two things about this correspondence especially arrested my attention. First there was a remarkable collection of postcards, most of them handmade, from both Tanner and Harwood, spanning many years, all of which featured a lighthouse. When asked what all these lighthouses signified, Gwen twinkled and said 'Oh Edwin and I were always going to run away together to a lighthouse. Of course, no-one ever believed us,' here she looked straight at me with her most beguiling smile, 'but we were.' The second thing I was curious about was the deep loathing she persistently expressed towards Tasmania, 'Turd Island', as she called it. Nearly two decades in Tasmania had not diminished her loathing and she wrote to Tanner that she faced her eighteen years in Tasmania 'with only the prayer that I won't die here'. This aspect of Gwen was something I was not inclined to probe, probably because I was still entranced with the place. However I was privately amused at the way the local writers and the provincial newspapers liked to picture Gwen as a champion of all things Tasmanian. They would be aghast to know that in private she said the whole place should be bulldozed, burned and sown with salt.

The first time I saw her outside Tasmania, at the Adelaide Writers Festival in the year *Bone Scan* won the poetry award, she was so elated and high spirited, simply bubbling with pleasure. It was not merely that she was beginning to receive her due which so delighted her, it was being away from

Tasmania, in a place where the weather was really hot. On another occasion she wrote to me after a visit to her 'blessed city', Brisbane, to receive an honorary doctorate. 'I sat by the Brisbane River and thought how I had been weeping by the waters of Babylon for forty-nine years.' As this was her third honorary doctorate, she joked to me that I should call her Dr Dr Dr Harwood and that she would have more gorgeous dressing gowns than any other old lady in the Sunset home.

We shared a late, indulgent breakfast in the restaurant at the top of the Regent during the Melbourne Writers Festival when she told me what it was like to meet again the man with whom she had been deliriously in love at nineteen years old. As she talked her lovely but careworn face was transformed into that of a young woman flushed rosy with – what was it? – lust, yes, that was it. Goodness, I thought, I now see how this woman writes such powerfully erotic and openly sexual poetry. Another time I saw her off the island we were both guests of the ASAL conference in Ballarat and we spent much of our time commiserating with one another about the dreadful cold and the impenetrable academic papers. During one such paper I was sitting beside Gwen, who scribbled a brilliant parody called The Dying Philosopher, in which she incorporated all the post-colonial jargon in perfect rhyme and iambic pentameter. I dissolved in fits of giggles when she tore out the two pages from her notebook and gave it to me, earning us both stern looks. Nevertheless when persuaded to read it at parody competition she won hands down, before going on to also win the ballroom dancing competition. She insisted I keep

the original which remains one of my treasures. As we flew
back into Hobart, Gwen confided that she could feel 'the old
Angst' settling on her soul again. She was fond of quoting Hal
Porter on the 'seedy terror' of Hobart and she seemed to
regard the community as having some inherent malevolence.
She always greatly encouraged my most outrageous assaults on
the smug provincialism of the place, but in retrospect I think
she was also trying to warn me that I could come to a bad end.

As indeed I did.

It began with a terrible weekend camp for the Fellowship
of Australian Writers, Tasmanian branch, (FAWT) where Gwen
and I were the tutors. It was a Baptist camp, spartan, frigid and
wowser. A nightmare. I got a splinter in my thumb from the
firewood I had to feed the boiler to get warm water and my
stomach rebelled against the grey mince stew we were provided at each meal. Persistent drizzle made for indoor
workshops so I encouraged my group to practise writing a dazzling opening paragraph which would grab the attention of the
reader and make the language sing. I quoted Karl Kraus who
said *let language be the divining rod that finds the sources
of thought.* After about thirty minutes one of the group
approached me with her paragraph. It began 'She sat in the
corner of the room with her arm around the dog'. I suggested
this was prosaic and dull. Who was this anonymous woman
and what was there about her that might engage the reader? I
asked. A few minutes later another attempt was offered:
'Marge sat on the veranda of the old cottage with her arm
around a blind dog'. On my return I entertained myself by

writing an editorial about this ordeal in *Island* magazine, of which I was the editor.

Gwen wrote to tell me this editorial caused consternation at the executive meeting of the 'Great Glorious and Correct FAWT' and she included a verbatim account of the discussion;

Old Dear: Have you read the editorial in *Island*?
GH: Really funny. I'll never forget the grey mince. Absolutely true.
Old Dear: But should she be allowed to say such things about a Baptist camp?
Another Old Dear: Gwen stoked the boiler too. I saw Gwen stoking the boiler and she didn't complain.
GH: I didn't get any splinters.
Old Dear: Well never mind that, did you see further down where it says about the dog?
GH: Absolutely hilarious. Incredible.
Old Dear: But cruel, cruel.
GH: Cruel? To whom? That writer was there to *learn*. Are you saying bad writing should be praised?
Old Dear: But should she have mentioned it?
GH: You sing in the tavern and you may get your ears cut off.

Gwen felt that may not be the end of the matter and concluded her letter 'if any boxes of chocolate come from the FAWT don't eat them carelessly. I saw a programme on Hitler in which his secretary said "he tested his poison capsule on the dog". Did he have his arm around it?'

It was by no means the end of the matter nor of my ill-judged assault on the wannabees who tried to control the literary scene in Hobart. I must say that Gwen was enthusiastically at my elbow all the time, though she herself was always sweetness personified in the face of persistent requests for her time and efforts to support 'local writing'. In private she would rail against it: 'slave labour that's what it is'. I was overseas when required to account for myself at a general meeting of the Tasmanian Writers Union, so Gwen agreed to read a statement I had written. She was shouted down – imagine, Gwen Harwood – before it was finished. Boy, did that make her angry! When I was unceremoniously sacked as editor of *Island* she was a rock of support for me and she encouraged me to sue, telling me that she had always wished for the courage to take on 'the mongrels'. Throughout that terrible time she would send me postcards with symbolic meaning and pointed messages, like this quote from the Psalms: 'I will follow upon mine enemies and overtake them: neither will I turn again till I have destroyed them.'

I think what I recognised in Gwen was the bad girl trying to get out. Perpetually a bad girl myself I had not appreciated how dangerous it might be to become a vehicle for her repressed naughtiness. She could be VERY naughty. She almost danced for joy that I was going to write about James McAuley for whom she had deeply ambivalent feelings. Curiously she refused to tell me much about him, but I now realise she knew better than almost anyone how the private man –

'the old devil' she called him – was very different from the public pose. As she wrote to another old friend of McAuley, few people were prepared to divulge anything about Jim 'except that contributing to the general piety', but my capacity for detective work would get to the real McAuley and that pleased her no end. Equally she knew I would get into terrible trouble doing it. She wasn't being simply mischievous. When she knew she was close to dying she invited me to have lunch with her for the sole purpose of telling me something very private and very significant about McAuley that she felt I should know.

Gwen Harwood did die in Tasmania as she had once dreaded. She did not go home to Queensland even though she controlled the management of her dying with magnificent determination. Our very last meeting was entirely orchestrated by Gwen who arranged for her son John, with whom I had gone to kindergarten, to drive her to Lower Snug to have lunch with my mother and me, as well as our friend and neighbour Lucy Frost. She insisted on bringing a home-made lunch and had that day baked fresh rolls for us. We had a lovely time and we all a laughed great deal. I understood that Gwen was saying goodbye to us and so I never contacted her again.

On reflection I don't believe she was unhappy to die in Tasmania. In the last few years she had taken huge pleasure in the cosmopolitan changes which had begun in Tasmania: new ideas and new people; fabulous food and wine. My most cherished memory of her is from 1993 on the Snug beach of my childhood. Although the wooden bridge over the rivulet and walkway was still there, the carbide works was long since dormant and the place was now transformed. To celebrate the anniversary of the visit of the French explorer Bruni D'Entrecasteaux the beach had been set up for a magnificent food and wine festival. All local produce but sponsored by the French consulate. Gwen was walking from stall to stall arm in arm with her oldest friend, Thomas Riddell. When she saw me her face lit up with that fabulous smile. 'You know Toto,' she called out to me, 'I don't think we are in Kansas any more.'

alexis wright

A FAMILY DOCUMENT

THERE IS A SAYING IN MY FAMILY which we use almost automatically to avoid potential unpleasantness – *Don't say anything*. I hear my Mother's voice – *If he turns up don't say anything*. Or, *Don't say anything, it is not worth it*. Or, *Don't say anything if anyone asks*. These are special words. If spoken by a senior relative, then these words are almost taken by the rest of our family as the word of law. So what happens with these words? I think I have inherited them. These words have buried a thousand crimes and a thousand hurts to save 'the peace' in the family. And why save the peace? Is peace more valid than speaking of hurt or has hurt become a substitute for truth? I think the answer is found in a place of the mind where peace of the family means having the privacy to be able to survive your own history with some sense of decency and worth.

I speak of my grandmother, known as Granny Ah Kup (Dolly Quinsen) who was not included in the Federation of Australia and she suffered from this deliberate exclusion of Aboriginal people in the Constitution of Australia.

Grandma was a Waanyi woman born on 14 November, 1903.

Throughout my life there have been a number of people who have had a powerful influence over my life. One was the late L. Lanley, a Waanyi leader of great gentleness and kindness, who was taken away from his traditional country to Mornington Island as a child. He died fighting for the rights of self-determination for his people. Another, was the late F. Clay, a very brave Kalkadoon leader who lived on Palm Island under the cruel laws of the Queensland *Aborigines Protection Act*. He also died fighting for the rights of Aboriginal people to be recognised in this country.

However, my main guide, nurturer and guardian was my grandmother. She was the person I had always turned to, ran away to, loved to be with, whom I felt gave me solace and space to daydream as a child. I had decided this from the time I was able to find my way to her place as a child of about three years old. My poor Mum lived smacked bang in the horror of the assimilation era of small town, North West Queensland. I avoided the creaking gate to avoid being caught by my Mother, and instead, climbed over the front fence of my parent's home in Cloncurry, a small town in north-west Queensland. I would sneak away from my poor, hard working Mother with heart pounding to run off down around the corner and down the streets heading towards Grandma's place. I believed I was in a strange, outback fairy land as I ran through the buffel grass and prickly bushes – a short cut, hidden from the gaze of nosey people until I got to the home run, down the road to Grandma's place, perhaps a kilometre or more from home. In the family nothing was said about it and peace prevailed, and in any case, my Mother frequently went down to Grandma's too. So Grandma's home was in some ways an extension of our own.

Grandma was born on an area of her traditional Waanyi land which in the closing decades of the nineteenth century had been illegally occupied by the colonialists and renamed Lawn Hills Station. Her mother was Opal Marinmarm whose parents were Cooloondoonowel (father) and Budjagwe (mother).*

In 1881 Dolly's mother was just a small child when she was 'taken' from her traditional Waanyi country by Frank Hann an early pastoralist. Hann was the then owner of Lawn Hills Station and notorious for his cruelty and brutal treatment of Aboriginal people. During the 1880s and 1890s under the policy of so-called 'pacification' many Aboriginal people living in the vicinity of Lawn Hills station were simply hunted down

---

* The spellings of these names were made in 1898 and are most likely incorrect. The names came from the wedding certificate for Opal and Sam Ah Bow, dated 1898, Lawn Hills Station.

and murdered. Young Aboriginal girls and women were cruelly procured for labour and sex on his property and disposed of as he saw fit. Hann and others of his ilk lived in virtual isolation from the laws and civil values of mainstream white society. They were a law unto themselves when it came to Aboriginal people. Shootings and acts of violence were commonplace. During the period between 1885 and 1896 when Frank Hann was on Lawn Hills, it has been estimated that between three hundred and four hundred Aboriginal people were shot.

This period of history is what Aboriginal people call the 'killing times' or 'wild times'. It was a time when tribes were scattered to the four winds, running for their lives and hiding in the more isolated areas of their country to get away from the white man's guns and horses. During this time there was a lot of movement of local tribespeople across the Queensland and Northern Territory border. Fleeing the killing fields of western Queensland, some Waanyi groups shifted west to the vicinity of the upper Nicholson River, the Barkly Tableland and further north.

Before colonisation Waanyi people travelled extensively across their traditional lands in what is now western Queensland and the north-eastern part of the Northern Territory. Regular ceremonial travel and trading extended from Turn Off Lagoon in the east to Alexandria, Cresswell Downs and Brunette Downs in the west. Ceremonies involved very large gatherings and all of these places fall within the boundaries of the Waanyi nation.

With the arrival of the pastoralists, the traditional trade

and ceremonial travel routes of Waanyi became escape routes for a people desperately seeking refuge from the murderous impact of white settlement. These trade routes, mapped by W. Roth, lead through country in the vicinity of Anthony Lagoon and Brunette Downs, south into Lawn Hills or north to Westmoreland, or through the mountainous country of the Nicholson River area to Turn Off Lagoon.

As the nineteenth century drew to a close increased pastoral activity in the Northern Territory forced many Waanyi east into Queensland to seek refuge. Many moved down the Nicholson River to Lawn Hills Creek and to the Turn Off Lagoon police depot, although, with the brutality of people like Hann, Lawn Hills was no longer a safe place. Hann believed that '*Blacks must obey and be taught to obey otherwise they will, as the saying is, "ride rough shod over one"*'. According to Trigger and Devitt, 'Hann (and his neighbours) fought to secure exclusive rights to land and water, but they required the labour of (some) Aboriginal people to successfully develop their enterprises. As this process of brutal confrontation and exploitation for labour continued, the scattered Waanyi found that their ancient trade routes were being taken over by the pastoralists to become their stock routes. With killings and violence becoming commonplace Waanyi people were no longer safe in their own lands.

According to my grandmother, the pastoralist Frank Hann was moving cattle across Waanyi lands when he 'found' young Opal and another little Waanyi girl sitting up a tree in the bush somewhere between Brunette Downs and

Lawn Hills. Hann's diary, quoted by Trigger and Devitt, notes
that while Hann was passing through Creswell Downs on
27 April, 1896, he recalls that fifteen years previously (i.e.
1881) he had 'caught Ophal the gin there'.*

In 1898, Opal married Sam Ah Bow. The marriage certificate states that Opal was born at Brunette Downs station
although no actual date of birth is given. This document raises
a question about Opal's birthplace. Brunette Downs was actually established in 1883, some two years after Hann says he
'caught' Opal. If Hann's date is correct then Opal was born
well before Brunette Downs came into existence.

During the 1880s when Cresswell Downs, Brunette
Downs and Alexandra were being established, a severe
drought forced the Barkly Tablelands pastoralists in the Territory to move their cattle east into the Nicholson River area.
Once again the Waanyi were forced to move and seek safety
within their vast territories.

Given Hann's notorious reputation it is hardly surprising
that his diaries contain few details or admissions of his brutal
deeds against the Waanyi people. One can only speculate then
about why two frightened little Waanyi girls were found up a

* The document goes on to say that Ophal was 15 at the time, but according to
Grandma's recollection, her Mother was a little girl when she was taken. Also,
according to the extensive research work undertaken by David Trigger, he has
established that the practice of selecting individuals to train as labourers and
servants was widespread and long-lasting. It was noted by Inspector Galbraith of
Normanton (1903) that plenty of children were separated from their parents,
and how they were separated is the subject of 'conjecture and surmise ... This
practice has been going on for years.' This was a practice of quietening down
'clearly identified' Aboriginal people so that they were more easily controlled.

tree, alone in the bush.* Where were their families? Why were they hiding in the tree? Were they survivors of one of Hann's murderous attacks on their people?

Did he take pity on them? What were his motives in bringing the two girls back? His diary actually uses the word 'caught' suggesting they had been hunted and captured rather than rescued. Given Hann's reputation the encounter appears to be the outcome of yet another untold tragedy.

Grandma's father, Sam Ah Bow, was a cook on Lawn Hills station. His father was a medical doctor in China. According to Grandma, Frank Hann gave Opal to Sam as a wife (marriage 5 May 1898, Lawn Hills Station) in appreciation for his services as though she was his to give away. Opal had already been married but Hann had for some reason intervened and taken her first husband away. No-one knows what happened to him. Opal's first son by this marriage whose name was Spider was taken by Hann along with a few other Aboriginal people to Western Australia when he left the Gulf. Some of these (presumably Waanyi) people ended up in the care of Daisy Bates (missionary). Spider eventually made his way back to Turn Off Lagoon.

Opal and Sam had seven children, two died young, and the oldest three were sent by their father back to China. No-one knows what became of them. It is likely that the reason why Sam sent the children out of the country was to avoid the policies of taking half-caste children away from their parents.

---

* Grandma's oral account was that her Mother Opal, when she was a little girl, along with another little girl, were found up a tree by Frank Hann.

Perhaps he was also reacting to the strong anti-Chinese feelings in Australia in the early part of the twentieth century which gave rise to the infamous White Australia Policy.

Under protest by Opal, her two youngest daughters, Dolly and Loma (Leon) were allowed to remain at home. Opal was a skilled bushwoman and midwife. She could ride a horse over long distances, apparently as well as any stockman, and delivered many babies in the area, including grandchildren from her two daughters. Nancy Wilson, a senior Waanyi woman and claimant, who lives on Mornington Island, has told me that Opal delivered her into the world. Through her role as midwife to many Waanyi women, Opal had a very close association to Waanyi society throughout the area. She also worked hard on the market garden at the Louie Creek sublease on Lawn Hills station which was purchased by Sam Ah Bow in 1907 for seventy pounds.* The garden produce was sold to the miners and stations in the area. Sam Ah Bow also bred horses and sold them to local stations as buggy horses.

Opal practised traditional law with other Waanyi women, including Grandma when she was a young woman, at Louie Creek. It is likely that they also participated in traditional law

* The garden was first established by a Chinese man called Tim See Too. He grew a large garden and banana plantation. He also built the horse-driven whim to water the area. These leases were then purchased by John Ingram on 19 June 1906 who apparently died within twelve months. However the following year in 1907, Ingram's brother visited the area to claim the land that was left to him. He then sold the land to Sam Ah Bow for the sum of seventy pounds in August 1907, but no record was documented of the transfer of the leases to Sam Ah Bow. In the 25 years until Sam's death in 1932, the Ah Bows had the market garden, and opened their home up to all travellers.

ceremonies in other places in the Lawn Hills area and surrounding Waanyi land on other stations in the area, i.e.,
Riversleigh. They travelled frequently to these places, as well
as to Burketown, and were well connected to other Aboriginal
families. They did what other Waanyi people were doing, continuing the practice of traditional law in their homelands,
despite the forced movement eastwards in the 1880s.

In 1918, at the age of fifteen, Grandma was married to
Johnny Ah Kup, after her father sold her to him. We know
nothing of how Grandma felt about being placed in this
marriage arrangement at such a young age. We also know nothing of how Opal felt about her husband's decision to sell his
young daughter for marriage. Given her own experience of an
arranged marriage under the control of the pastoralist Hann, it
is likely that Opal would have felt she had little choice in such
matters. Such was the way of things at the time. During the earlier years of their marriage Grandma and Johnny Ah Kup
worked on several stations such as Gregory Downs, Riversleigh,
Avon Downs and Camooweal. They also continued to work the
market garden at Louie Creek and had eleven children.

For Grandma and her husband it was hard work trying to
make a living from the Louie Creek garden. Conditions were
far from salubrious, even though living beside the spring-fed
waters of the Lawn Hills gorge and the surrounding rainforest
type vegetation and wildlife gives the impression of living in
paradise. Grandma grew up with Waanyi, Garawa and Gang-
galida people and those of her generation still living remember
her well. Some of the Waanyi people who are now deceased,

remembered Grandma as a Waanyi woman and sister. I remember some of these people were the late Jock Pedro, C. Dick, T. George, Cora Peters (tribal sister) and L. Lanley. One living Waanyi woman of Grandma's generation is Liddy Peters who lives in Mount Isa. Grandma used to call the late Mrs Ah Kit (Camooweal) and Mrs Turner (Cloncurry), and Mrs Yamagushi of Burketown now living in Mount Isa her old sisters in the traditional way. It was only the people of this older generation who called her sister. Everyone else in the Aboriginal community including close family in north-west Queensland, either called her Mum, Grandma or Aunty, and never ever by her first name.

When Sam Ah Bow died at Louie Creek in 1932, the family were unable to maintain the work required to run the garden. Unlike his father-in-law, Johnny Ah Kup did not seem to have the same high level of gardening interest and the family's situation worsened. Their problems were compounded when the sublease for Louie Creek was not transferred into Grandma's name although records show that the Ah Bows had paid the lease rent until Sam died.* The family were also under regular surveillance from Mr Thornton, Protector of Aborigines at Gregory Downs who, according to official correspondence, did not have a high regard for Johnny Ah Kup whom he accused of being a liar, selling his daughters

---

* My cousin Phyllys Ah Kit has more substantial documentation of the family's history at Louie Creek from the considerable work she had done by collecting oral accounts from Grandma and by researching archival documents concerning the family.

and harbouring Aborigines and undesirables. Thornton was considering whether to place the children on Mornington Island or Doomadgee.

At the time there was considerable collaboration between the local Protector of Aborigines, police, pastoralists or other locals in the area regarding the affairs of mixed race families. Control was systematic, and applied through the heavy-handed use of *The Aboriginals Protection and Restriction of the Sale of Opium Acts*, 1897 to 1934. As well as these pressures on the family, Louie Creek dried up for the first time in living memory. The family had strong suspicions that a Frenchman, Albert De Lestang, at nearby Adels Grove (Frenchmen's Garden), had diverted the creek from flowing past the Louie Creek garden to remove Grandma's garden from being in competition with his own.* In 1936, due to lack of water, the family were forced to move to Camooweal. Five years later Opal died there at approximately ninety years of age at the Camooweal Hospital, at 1.30pm, 9 August, 1941. She was buried at the Camooweal cemetery on the same day.

The Ah Kup family had moved to Cloncurry in the mid-1930s and this is where Johnny Ah Kup died before many of us were born. He is buried in the Chinese cemetery next to the Coppermine Creek crossing on the left hand side of the Mount Isa road outside of Cloncurry. Grandma once located his grave for me by pointing to a branch of a gum tree which she said pointed to his grave.

* Recollections by my Mother, Alice Wright.

Grandma did not read or write and when she lived in Cloncurry, she worked at a hotel washing sheets by hand to support her large family as well as taking in other people's ironing at home. For many years she lived in a small corrugated iron house without electricity and heated the iron on the wood fuel stove for which she also chopped the wood. The family lived with kerosene and carbide lamps at night, often sitting outside for hours on old kero drums under the stars, Grandma telling stories, and drinking tea before going to bed.

On one occasion Grandma fought the landlord and town authorities who tried to make her move from her rented property, a corrugated iron humpy on a large block on the edge of town, until they backed down and allowed her to stay. This property was eventually bought by her youngest son who erected a better house for her, and she stayed there until her health became a family concern and she moved to Mount Isa.

Grandma believed in the natural world and family. It was these two things that mattered most to her. For Grandma all answers to the realities of life were to be found in natural phenomena, for example, she believed that the place and time that children are conceived and born shapes their personalities and how they live their lives. When I was a child I often heard her speak about my uncles or aunties and their likeness to some behaviour of their totem (animal or spirit being) which coincided with her pregnancy or their birth.

I also remember times when she had to borrow a few dollars because she had run short of money before pension day. She would not take more than a few dollars. Then the following week she would always return with the few dollars, still tied up in the end of a handkerchief, insisting on giving it back. When you refused to take the money, she would insist by saying, 'No, you need it.' She had not even spent the money because she did not like to use your money. Every time anyone in the family visited Grandma over the years she would always bring out the many photograph albums she kept that were full of photos of members of the family. She would go through all of these photos just telling you who everyone was, their names, what relative they were to us. Then on Christmas Day all of the family came to Grandma's place and the lunch would be served up under the mango trees.

I had never known her to turn a person away in her life. She was a relentless visitor to other families, or she was forever calling passing people to her home for a chat. She stopped in the street for anyone, going out of her way to do so, simply because she was interested in their welfare and the plight they all shared. She could never afford to give much to others materially, but she touched them, and she sympathised, and everyone loved her for giving a gift more valuable than money, her time.

I spent a lot of time with my Grandma as a child and I know these things to be true, just as I know she walked all over the river beds and bush outside of Cloncurry as I often went with her and sat with her while she fished, daydreamed, or sought out a cup of tea with strange people camped by themselves. She made a large garden at her Cloncurry home where she grew vegetables such as Chinese cabbage, parsnips, carrots and other Asian vegetables as well as grapevines. She also grew flowers such as petunias, zinnias and everlasting daisies, nanny goat flowers and other old-fashioned flowers that could grow well in the extreme climate of Cloncurry. The flower bed had a border of brown bottles half buried upside-down. Tom Thumb tomatoes grew by themselves in her yard as well as rosellas for jam. She loved to experiment and tried her hand at growing cotton, peanuts and anything else that took her fancy or because someone gave her seeds or cuttings to try out. She grew her own mango trees from seed in tins she collected from the rubbish dump. In fact, she had many pot plants in tins collected from the dump and it seemed she was always moving these plants from the shade of one tree to another. Her yard contained an assortment of trees, all of which she grew, such as cedars, fig, oleander, chinky apple tree, banana and poinciana trees. Not one weed grew in her yard because she would wake up early every morning to rake the yard and to remove any weed, chick weed or buffel grass, that showed any sign of budding its head out of the ground. All of this was removed no matter how hard the ground was, or even that more weeds would grow from the seeds that flew into her yard from across her fence. All of the weeds she collected were fed to her chooks, ducks and bush turkey down the back.

She was fond of animals and at one stage she had three dogs. In particular, I remember Widgee and Goofy. Goofy, a brown and white spotted dog, she told off one day for digging too many holes under the mango tree and the dog got up and walked out of the yard and went to live with the Dargon family next door. He never ever returned to her place again. Apart from these things, Grandma was a person who lived simply. She never had a lot in terms of material goods or money. She liked to cook cabbage stew and on Sunday she cooked a roast or corned beef and a treacle pudding with custard. She walked in the hot sun to town every day with her shopping buggy and came home with whatever groceries she needed, and always after spending considerable time talking to whoever she met along the way. Then she had a rest in the afternoon, sometimes on the iron beds under the mango trees at the back before cooking the evening meal before it got dark. Grandma slept permanently outside when Aunty Sylvia died. Aunty Sylvia was very shy of people and had lived with Grandma most of her life. Her death deeply troubled Grandma, as it did when other members of her family died who were younger than herself.

Grandma was a person who was always interested in new ideas particularly if it was anything to do with making life better around the home. For instance, she liked new types of torches, recipes on packages and new types of contraptions to capture cockroaches or flies. She was most impressed with these things and she would love telling everyone about it, often saving the packaging, so she could show it to others.

We shared a love of music, and when I was a child, I used to love the evenings when everyone sat outside talking and I played the wind-up gramophone my mother had given Grandma. It was my job to select the music amongst a stack of old country and western 78s. I played Tex Owens type music,

I especially remembered the 'Cattle Call' as a favourite.

I remember making Grandma a papier-mâché cat which she placed in her vegetable garden she tried to establish in Mount Isa in Eric's backyard. She said the cat was good because it scared the birds away. She tried very hard to create a garden and to grow trees again but the ground was very hard and full of gravel and the chemical discharge flowing off the stack from the mine. It was a wonder that anything grew at all.

Grandma attached no importance to being Waanyi other than it being a state of being. She also acknowledged her Chinese inheritance, never seeing or judging people in terms of colour be they black, white, or any colour in between. What she looked for in people was which family they belonged to and she was very good at picking family resemblances. She spoke the Waanyi language and it was always her dream for favourable circumstances to arise in her life so that she could return to her beloved Louie Creek. However, with all roads into Louie Creek closed or kept locked by the cattle station owner of Lawn Hills until the opening of the national park in the 1980s, it was an impossible dream for Aboriginal people with no means of transport to achieve their goal of being reunited with their homelands. Grandma was in her eighties then but that did not deter her from making two family trips back to 'visit' the Lawn Hills (National Park).

This was her dream and she spoke about Louie Creek often, for decades in fact, long before what we call her dream to return home became a term like 'land rights', or even 'native title'. And also long before the competition for power over resource rights that sadly we now see taking place, where the illegal and wrongful interpretation of Indigenous rights perpetrated by present-day governments make many of us fail in the great struggle common to all of us – to live as a decent human being.

Grandma's way of transmitting knowledge was to tell the stories about the country. These were the stories that arise from nature. She knew how to explain the natural world in terms of traditional knowledge that she learned at Lawn Hills where Louie Creek is situated. Like other Aboriginal people, Grandma collapsed history and assimilated the remote Dreamtime into the present in order to explain her attachment to country.*

I, and many of my cousins grew up with the vision Grandma instilled into us of our traditional country. It is through following her way that this family has been represented in the battle for indigenous rights for country. In my

---

* Dr M. Reay, in the Borroloola claim described the concept of common descent from a common mythic ancestor as: 'Aborigines collapse history and assimilate the remote Dreamtime into the present. Transformations of quasi-ancestral beings are visible in the landscape. Ceremonies re-enact their adventures and their paths are recorded in song. The remote past is ever present. An individual's connection to it is his Dreamings and the land in which his Dreamings are located. The quasi-ancestral beings he shares with his father and the land establish his descent through spirits located in that land from the first people those beings originated.

'… when people perform increase rites, singing sacred songs and acting out totemic dramas, they, so to say, install themselves as ancestral beings – they actually become totemic ancestors themselves by putting to use the knowledge that they have acquired though long trials of initiation into sacred lore. … And since the dead, to their normal human aspect, are to a large extent expunged from history, all that remains of them are the mythic identities that they once acted out in ritual. Hence, the dreaming is at once ancient and rarely further back than two generations, since the dead are constantly assimilated to the mythological identity of the country.'

own case, I have tried through the work I have undertaken over many years to help protect our country and in my work as an author. My eldest daughter, Tate Narritjin (Evening Star), was given her bush name by the late Cora and Gully Peters of Mornington Island soon after she was born. My youngest daughter Lily, Alice, Anna, Badjawa, is named after her grandmothers and her great, great, great grandmother. The late Paddy Bell, a senior Waanyi traditional owner had one time told me that Badjawa means the Wild Plum tree.

In many of us, Grandma's vision is still firmly planted in our minds and the true guidance from the senior holders of traditional law in our Waanyi homelands is our inheritance. If we are to survive, their law should flow down to all of us, so that every Waanyi has the opportunity to learn more about our traditional domain and be given the opportunity to take up the responsibilities for country that flows from residing within our ancient boundaries. In the end, it will be from the inclusion of the skills and potential of all Waanyi that our nation and homelands will survive and grow in a positive way.

Grandma Nulayanma passed away peacefully on 4 August 1999.

WESTERLY

STORIES · POEMS · ARTICLES · REVIEWS

JUNE, 1985

elizabeth jolley

PETER COWAN: THE CRITERION AND THE PRINCIPLE

PACKED IN THE CLAUSTROPHOBIC VAN in the strong scent of chewing gum, deodorant and sweat, the conversation which appears to be desultory at first becomes loaded. The girls fail in their first attempt to get the van driver to stop the van. He has, as well, declined the doubtful pleasure of a double screw at the side of the road.

Windmills, Lee said you never fell off one of them?
Fell off?
Not so far.

Always a first time.
Thanks I'll watch it.
I mean, they turn around. You get in the way up there
could be bad.

Quickly they think of the unavoidable reason for stopping the
van and getting him out of it. In this story there is an overwhelming sense of disaster. The dialogue is economical, it is
sinister and leads directly to the last paragraph in the story. The
van driver's ultimate confusion is mirrored in his own reflection about the ants. 'But at least it was wet for them' he
thought, seeing the pattern of their movement broken … The
symbolism of the mobiles being thrown out of the moving van
suggests a deeper level in the story, a kind of desperation not
acknowledged by the girls. A pathetic attempt to show their
freedom and being their own 'Boss' when they are obviously
caught up in a world, a tough and ugly world from which, it
seems, impossible to get free. This underlying unhappiness,
loneliness and fear is felt deeply by Peter Cowan and can be
found in other stories. He does not offer compassion in an
obvious sentimental way of writing.

Some years ago I read Peter Cowan's story *Mobiles* (published FACP, 1979) to a 'Mature Age Enjoyment of Literature
Class' at the Fremantle Arts Centre. There were ten women
and two men in the class.

I explained some of Peter Cowan's special ways of writing, the lack of inverted commas for dialogue, for example,
and his economy of words and how much every word was nec-

essary for the material and the flavour of the prose. For example, in a few words, Peter Cowan has the atmosphere of the loneliness of a road in the outback of Western Australia on the page. The reader could feel the heat and the silence, the apparent emptiness.

The story was about two girls hitch-hiking and having been footloose and restless they centre their intention of trying to 'get a lift', a truckie earlier having dropped them – a wise man! Because a transporter roars along the road the girls will probably get picked up. The van driver does give them a lift at great cost to himself and his own life … the students were asked to comment, if they wished to give a wide picture.

The women, two of them together, an angry chorus saying that the girls were no good that they had been to good expensive schools, their parents going without things they needed and these girls just wasting themselves and the goodness of their parents, they ought to be punished, these girls, probably were running after some no good man and all the time breaking their mothers' hearts. And so on …

It was my first experience of what could be called Readers' Preconceived Opinions. There was nothing in the text to support and show what the two students were saying.

I include this because there are a number of people who read and react from prejudicial and incorrect attitudes in advance of understanding or even trying to understand. This tendency towards the detrimental overlooks all that the writer is trying to show in his poems or short stories and, of course, his novels and literary articles and reviews.

The flesh of animals who feed excursively is allowed to have a higher flavour than that of those who are cooped up. May there not be the same difference between men who read as their taste prompts, and men who are confined in cells and colleges to stated tasks.

This was said by Dr Samuel Johnson in 1728 and, as a profound truth, is quoted by people who love books and reading, at the present time.

The book *Westerly 21*, edited by Peter Cowan and Bruce Bennett, was published by the Freemantle Arts Centre Press in 1978. A press which began to bring the names of new writers in Australia to an audience of readers who were waiting for the highly flavoured flesh of new books.

Peter Cowan and Bruce Bennett, both at the time, from the English Department of the University of Western Australia, were and are interested in books and reading and writing and devoting their time and energy to be on the lookout (through their editorial work on the *Quarterly Journal Westerly*), for freshly written material, short stories, non-fiction essays, dignified reviewing and poems. Literary articles and the reviewing of books from England and America and across Australia presented the editors with endless work to be done as well as the preparation for their lectures. As editors they were meticulous and enthusiastic. A great help to new writers in Western Australia.

Peter Cowan, himself a writer of short fiction and novels, wrote the following in his introduction to the book *Westerly 21*.

Through fat and lean years it provides a record of Austalian short story writers at the leading edges of their craft, shaping their different materials to give them significance.

The editors said that they were looking for material they felt to be worthwhile in itself, they wanted material 'that will come alive off the page'.

The editors wanted, in the anthology, to show changes that had taken place over the years. Changes in ideas, changes in critical attitude, change in the form of the short story and in poetry. They encountered difficulties because writers themselves change. Many writers published years ago in *Westerly* (the Journal) have come to fresh ideas, and new ways of writing.

Does it matter if the writer changes? Who can answer that sort of question? Certainly it matters if, after writing interesting stories, he starts to write incredibly dull ones.

It is interesting to wonder if it matters if a writer changes. The change which reflects development, and which, in itself reflects our own changing society. There are many questions and statements here. One question might be about the changes in attitude in society. The writer's reflection on present-day changes, with some thoughts being too sad and too difficult to offer pleasure and relaxation when reading, is a statement too difficult for a question here.

The literary journals housed in the English Departments of the universities across Australia provided lecturers and teachers with valuable reading experience and, for writers emerging, the journals were the streets for them to follow in meeting other writers, both established and new writers. Peter Cowan had a high standard for writing from Western Australia. He never spoke without first thinking. He was in those days a quiet (almost shy) man. His handwriting was meticulous and enhanced the rejection slips. If you, as a writer, received an acceptance slip for some submitted work you know that he really meant acceptance. He did not pretend an acceptance, similarly the writer could accept the rejection. Peter Cowan did not, he told me, go out to lunch. It took up too much time, he said, and I understood that he was making use of ounces of time when I was probably eating and busy wasting precious time in talking. The writer has to learn that writing will not do its own work!

New work was submitted to *Westerly* for consideration. Peter Cowan did not readily accept new work, having a criterion always on his mind, the most responsible reviews, the freshest ideas for fiction, the most musical prose and the same for poetry. The Criterion and the Principle were very important and were part of the possibility for acceptance. It was said, on occasion, that far more people submitted their work for possible publication than subscribed to the Journal.

Peter Cowan always said that, as Editor, he was always on the lookout for a high standard of work. They were looking for material they felt to be worthwhile, in itself, as Peter Cowan said himself, material that 'came alive off the page'.

The literary journals, needed so much by the emerging

writer, were brought about by people like Peter Cowan. People who loved their 'part of the land' (and city), people like Peter Cowan, in his writing of short fiction, novelist and critic. And his ability to read and advise a new writer.

Peter Cowan gave me a present. I had never seen his book of short stories *Drift* (published during the war, 1944, by Reed and Harris, Melbourne and Adelaide).

As he gave it to me he said he was sorry that it was coming to pieces, it was the war, he said, paper was impossible, it did not keep (if you managed to get some). How would I mind at all in the face of this lovely present? It is the brown of the paper, just bits coming off, the stories are all present. As well as saying he was sorry, he wrote it on a label which is stuck in the book. The stories are richly flavoured with the characters – many predicaments and rites of passage before and during the war in Australia! The war for me was in England with closeness to Europe and to the British Isles – Scotland, Ireland and Wales north and south.

The flavour of Peter Cowan's present, the flavour of the material, the art of this book, *Drift*, gave me thoughts which might never have come into my thoughts because the experience, though similar, could not be the same. From this book I learned, among other things, I learned to take more experience from my reading and I found this happened also with other books of Peter Cowan's.

All kinds of human behaviour are in poems and stories. Like the painter, whose mind is a storehouse packed with sunsets, the writer's mind is stored with sunsets upon sunsets, the writers mind is stored with impressions and with sights and sounds and meanings which deal with reverence and with responsibilities and with love. The writer is concerned with all things which evoke the playful, the ridiculous, the amusing, the mad, the angry, the pathetic, the hopeful and the tender. His heart and mind are an eternal profusion from which he struggles to bring out some kind of simple beauty and order. (William Wordsworth paraphrased.)

Readers who care to compare earlier stories with the later ones will see too how Cowan reflects, with a clear vision, our own changing attitudes and behaviour.

Gerald Bullett said, in his *Biography of George Eliot*, that a character in fiction, if it is to have any life, must be created and not merely remembered. Peter Cowan does remember and record and, at the same time, he is creating fiction and showing the reader an inner vision of human life in addition to the external details of the places where this life is lived. He acknowledges the plain fact that a man can perish very quickly if he is lost and alone in places not very far from human habitation. He is well aware of the harshness of the Western Australian climate and the ease with which an individual can lose his way. These facts, looked at symbolically, fit our own muddled wanderings and attempts at communication. In spite of the dangers, many of the characters find solace in the solitude. 'The images of rock, gravel, dust and the deserted mine-head poppets, the endless scrub ringed with conical hills, split by ravines and gullies', are the places where his characters come within the possibilities of making some kind of deep self-discovery. He seems able in his writing to bring about a kind of reconciliation between the external, as just described, and the internal, that of attitudes, imaginations and emotions, the one seeming to offer some release for the realisation of the other.

From the port of Fremantle, on the west coast, the flat sand-plains encompassing the city of Perth stretch for about fifteen miles to an escarpment. Over and beyond these ridges of low hills there is a mixture of rural land, which has been cleared for farming, and the bush. Michael, in the title story of *The Empty Street*, comes upon the possibilities of evasion and escape, briefly putting off what he must ultimately face. He is now a stranger, an intruder, but is kindly received. At the lonely house, and with the woman who lives there, he experiences consolation. The brittle values of his suburban existence fall away as he helps to plant seedlings.

He worked without haste, there was only the new soil he had prepared, the feel of it beneath his fingers, friable, the thin slips of the greyish stems as he set them, the slow changes of light as the trees along the rise grew deeper in colour.

For a short time he is in a place of retreat, of sanctuary. He finds the Horatian vision, a final gift perhaps:

Abandon the wearisome plenty, the pile
that approaches the soaring clouds;
leave wondering at the smoke,
the money, the din of wealthy Rome …
He lives well on a little whose family

salt-cellar shines amidst a modest table …
… you can assuage
your small Gods with Rosemary crowns
and delicate Myrtle garlands ...

Like Ibsen and Chekov, Cowan asks questions and never offers answers, and he never pronounced judgment.

Many of Peter Cowan's characters, in his earlier stories, can be seen now as the forerunners of our own society. To some this may be an unwanted truth.

Drift, the title story of Cowan's 1944 collection, reflects the changes which were accelerated in the Second World War. Young people who were restless in lonely rural communities began even more to want to leave the farming life. They wanted to get right away from the land, the clearing of which had claimed the energy and sometimes the lives of their parents and grandparents.

E.M. Forster, in the novel *Where Angels Fear To Tread*, speaks of the wonderful physical tie which binds the parents to the children; and – by some strange irony – it does not bind us children to our parents.

In the story *Drift*, both the son and the daughter, in spite of their father's love for them, and in spite of his long life of creating the farm for them, both the son and the daughter have dreams of getting away to the war.

It was lunchtime. In the morning the Bren-gun carriers had been through the fields … 'Wish I had been in one of them,' the boy said …

That's what I'm going to try to get into …

The father tries to put forward the good reasons for remaining on the farm. Soldiers have to have food, he tells them. To him, in spite of the remoteness and the heavy work, the farm is the place to be.

Forster's physical tie is here, unacknowledged, changed into something else. The father, inarticulate in his love for his children, sees what is for him, the greater need beyond this – love – for them to stay.

The father in the story *Drift*, the father and farmer has to acknowledge the fact that his son wants to go to the war. He has been accepted. In a brief exchange the father, unable to explain how much he needs and loves his son says, 'I been here thirty years since my old man died', he gestures his hand towards the paddocks, the green deep in the fading light. The boy's eyes were restless.

'Don't matter,' the man said. He pushed the gate open. 'I'll bring the cows in.'

Peter Cowan's characters are often silent, saying the least on occasions where other authors' characters might well hold forth.

When discussing his work with Wendy Jenkins, Peter Cowan said, after a remark about the silences in his work, that this sort of landscape is a landscape of silences and spaces. He said that it could not be talked about in a 'language which is lavish and over-ornamented … You have to try and find a prose that expresses it within itself.'

During the discussion, Peter Cowan made a revealing remark,

> If you want to write things which everybody will read and enjoy, you write something a little different. I wouldn't expect that my work would get a wide audience. I'd be very surprised if it did.

Wendy Jenkins, writing about the novel, *The Colour of the Sky*, writes,

> This novel is the work of a man who has thought and felt much. The reader who approaches it with proper humility may sometimes feel repelled and may, at times, feel lost. To read with perseverance is to find imaginative power and deep insight and compassion.

brian matthews

HANSON

HENRY LAWSON was one of the greatest writers this country has produced, even if the body of work on which such an evaluation is based was in the end regrettably slim. In his own time, it was his 'Australianness' that tended to be valued above the understated, allusive prose and the magnificent, deceptively effortless flow of narrative. This was neither an unreasonable nor an unsophisticated judgement by contemporary readers who found in Lawson's spare and fragile stories a convincing rendition of their own perceptions and unarticulated feelings about, among other things, the nature of the land they lived in. When they read the opening sentences of 'In A Dry Season' – 'Draw a wire fence and a few ragged gums and add some scattered sheep running away from the train. Then you'll have the bush all along the New South Wales western line from Bathurst on' – they felt the exquisite frisson of utter rightness, that sense of surprised familiarity that is part of the appreciation of art. Lawson's unerring observation, his 'hammer blow' of simplicity and truth, still resonate more than a hundred years after the publication of *While the Billy Boils*. Which is why, for better or worse, his name and his art are the focus of many claims and the site of many arguments about what it is to be Australian, what Australia – that place and that idea for which he wrote with 'all his heart' – actually means. As a result, he comes to mind, or is brought to mind, sometimes in the strangest company but none the less evocatively for all that …

Pauline Hanson's ill-orchestrated, abrasive and stumble-footed return to the political scene in the new century is a reminder of how bizarre was her original entry onto that crowded and ever more tawdry stage and raises again the question whether she is a wild and walking aberration or a version of something even vaguely recognisable in our past.

In her maiden speech to Parliament, she said, 'My view on issues is based on common sense and my experience as a mother of four children, as a sole parent and as a business-woman running a fish and chip shop'; and, later in the same speech: 'I may be only "a fish and chip shop lady", but some of these economists need to get their heads out of the textbooks and get a job in the real world. I would not even let one of them handle my grocery shopping.' She considered herself, she said by way of conclusion, 'an ordinary Australian who wants to keep this great country strong and independent'. To some extent, these quite important statements were overrun by her more sensational claims about Asian immigration and the Asianisation of Australia which, with their racist overtones, rang many more alarm bells and flushed out more ambivalent supporters than did snippets of autobiography.

Yet Pauline Hanson's explanation of how her views were formed were illuminating about One Nation and its adherents. However much its immediate provenance lay in rebellion against the legacy of the never-very-clearly-delineated 'elites', the sense of grievance evinced by One Nation members and cohorts seemed to have its origins further back, and my first thought was that One Nation represented the latest chapter in the long history of Australian anti-intellectualism. Hanson's citing of 'common sense' as against rarefied specialism; gritty at-the-coal-face experience as against heads-in-textbooks; hardship and struggle as against the easy ride disjoined from 'the real world', constitutes a familiar litany. It is a chant which attains high volume in hard times, when 'intellectuals' seem both impossibly impractical and outrageously privileged; just as calls for the removal or debarring of 'foreigners' ebb and flow in harmony with perceptions that native-born (that is, in Hanson-speak, white) Australians are being done out of their rights (to work, space, profit, identity, etc).

As an expositor of this position, Hanson had an unlikely predecessor in Henry Lawson: a comparison can be instructive given Lawson's status as one of the interpreters of our cultural and historical heritage. During the 1890s, Lawson several times expressed his conviction that his works were misunderstood or had suffered undue neglect. On one of these occasions he wrote a few verses entitled 'The Uncultured Rhymer to His Cultured Critics'. This outburst was probably provoked by John Le Gay Brereton – critic, academic, dedicated bookman, a good friend to Lawson and a very strong supporter of his work. Brereton incurred Lawson's displeasure with a simple and well-intended suggestion that the young poet should widen his range of literary reference by broader reading. Lawson's response was surprisingly strident, a sneer in verse:

> My cultured friends, you have come too late
>   With your bypath nicely graded.
> I've fought thus far on my track of Fate
>   And I'll follow the rest unaided.

This 'track of Fate' he sees as being interrupted by the interposition of a 'college gate': 'Must I be stopped by a college gate/On the track of life encroaching?' It's as if you're strolling along through the countryside free to follow your own course, as you should be in a new, egalitarian land like Australia, when suddenly your way is blocked by unwarranted gates and fences, unjustifiable territorialism. Thus Lawson manages to conflate unacceptable privilege with knowledge and education. The poem ends with four lines that are quite famous in Australia and often quoted:

I leave you alone in your cultured halls
   To drivel and croak and cavil;
Till your voice goes further than college walls
   Keep out of the tracks we travel.

It is not difficult to imagine with what intent, on what occasions and by whom these lines are quoted: they are a stick to beat 'the intellectuals' with and they have the great virtue of seeming to make and to prove the case in the one quotable coup. Here are much the same arguments as those deployed by Pauline Hanson: a comparison of the 'University of Hard Knocks' with the ivory tower of intellectual privilege and a clear implication about the two sharply opposed kinds of graduates that issue from them. The Lawson of 'The Uncultured Rhymer to his Cultured Critics' would obviously not have entrusted his grocery shopping to Brereton or his mates. Lawson's depiction of himself – by implication in the poem and in more detail in a famous letter to the *Bulletin* – is not unlike Hanson's. He describes himself, with reasonable though not complete accuracy, as a 'shy, ignorant lad from the bush, under every disadvantage arising from poverty and lack of education'. 'I started,' he goes on, 'with implicit faith in human nature and a heart full of love for Australia.' He places great store by writing 'for' Australia, writing in his country's interests: and it's true to say that, as his work evolved, it certainly was, at its best, stitching painfully together a particular, memorable and extraordinary vision of the nation and its people. His dedication to that literary-nationalist cause, he complains more and more explicitly, had not met with its just rewards.

On the question of anti-Asian racism, too, Lawson and Hanson seem to find common ground. Lawson's version, directed in his case of course at the Chinese, was actually quite amiable, as far as such references can be amiable, and thoroughly of its time. But the pressure of the times is not, as we well know, an acceptable excuse; some people, after all, still managed to protest against the tide of popular opinion, as Henry Reynolds has so splendidly demonstrated in *This Whispering in Our Hearts*. In contemporary Australia the consciousness of society has been raised on questions of race, but it is still possible, as Hanson has shown, to espouse publicly a racist position and as a result feed off the vigorous incipient racism within our society if you're prepared, as she and her supporters seem to be, to tough out the ensuing uproar. (A good demonstration of successful consciousness-raising on race is found in AFL football where, as a result of rigorous education, counselling and campaigning, it is now entirely out of the question, practically unthinkable, for a player to risk uttering a racist slur: nothing – not the heat of the moment nor the tension of battle – will excuse such behaviour; if you do it, you're '*gone*'.) In the 1890s, it was difficult not to accept prevailing 'soft' racism; as for aggressive racism – in the form of massacres and callous exploitation – to use a metaphor constantly employed during the nineteenth century in Australia, 'a veil was drawn' over such horrors and embarrassments. Even the founding fathers wrote racial exclusion into the Constitution provoking scarcely a whimper of dissent let alone outrage. So, throwaway racist utterances are there to be found in Lawson and his contemporaries. There are Banjo Paterson's shearers who decamp when Chinese are employed in the sheds:

So it's shift boys, shift, for there isn't any doubt
It's time to make a move when the leprosy's about.

And there's the Aboriginal in Lawson's 'The Drover's Wife' who builds a hollow woodheap for the struggling woman; and innumerable and invariably comic Chinese storekeepers; and Harry, the Aboriginal rouseabout working for Joe Wilson, of whom Joe says '[he] came sidling along the wall as if he were afraid someone was going to hit him – poor little devil! I never did.' And so on.

But if, in line with the times he lived in, Lawson didn't give much thought to the issue of race, he did give a great deal of thought both to the art he so longed to excel at and its relationship with the country he loved and lived in. Lawson tried desperately to get himself an education but circumstances and the fact that he wasn't all that good at formal learning defeated him. Nevertheless, he imbibed Australian cultural and political history from his mother, her friends, and various workmates and writers: as a young man he knew very well where he stood on the matter of Queen Victoria's Jubilee, the Women's Movement and Republicanism, for example. And his unerring eye for the congruence between landscape and lives and for the subtle shifts and gradations in human relationships allowed him gradually to build a body of work in which was proclaimed not the truth of history or scholarship but the truth of fiction – a potent truth and a durable one. As well, Lawson was interested in grappling with the connection between his imaginative world *on the page* and the actual 'metropolis of the great scrubs' beyond the cities; he wanted to gauge the worth of his literary *métier* – realism. Though not by any means a theorist or essayist, Lawson did in fact make some pronouncements on this question in articles that were rough and ready enough but which have come to be recognised as important indications of his views on literary realism and what he was trying to do himself. For example, in 'Some Popular Australian Mistakes', Lawson lists ways in which description of the Australian landscape is distorted by Anglocentric tradition and vocabulary (a river 'is not a broad shining stream … it is … a string of muddy waterholes', and so on); and he reaches this conclusion:

> We wish to heaven that Australian writers would leave off trying to make a paradise out of the Out Back Hell … What's the good of making a heaven of a hell when by describing it as it really is, we might do some good for the lost souls there?

Lawson's idea that you wrote for Australia, that your work, if properly pitched, might benefit and illuminate the country and its people, is here again explicit. In his exasperation, he may very well have had in mind (as his great contemporary, Joseph Furphy, assuredly did), Henry Kingsley's popular, relentlessly anglophile, colonial romance, *The Recollections of Geoffry Hamlyn* (1859), in which a famous descriptive passage of the Australian inland begins with the words *A new heaven and a new earth!* and, after an avalanche of glens, woods, downs, boskey uplands, 'not untuneful birds', and other northern hemisphere literary landscape paraphernalia, concludes: *We are in Australia!* Well, it wasn't the Australia Lawson knew, since, for one thing, he saw no heavenly ingredient (though Hell got a guernsey often enough); moreover, he had a developing Australian brand of the English language to capture the sights he saw and the sounds he heard and, writing forty years on from Kingsley, was not in debt to the terminology of English landscape description in order to evoke an entirely different scene. Indeed, he was forging a new utterance and, in relative isolation, tuning a quite different note.

So Lawson, while very much a 'University of hard knocks' graduate, and in some ways proudly so, was not anti-intellectual. On the contrary, he sought to be educated, he understood the force of the artistic in ordinary mundane existence, he placed great store by knowledge, education and erudition (he apologised to Brereton for his intemperate rejoinder and asked him to overlook the 'uncultured rhymer' as an aberration!). He illuminated Australians to themselves not by scholarly reference or discourse but by creative intuition allied with an eerily pre-modernist, spare and cryptic prose style that he worked very hard to perfect and the puzzling deterioration of which he regarded as the tragedy of his life. When he lamented not long before his death and after the long and shocking decline of his fortunes and his writing career, that he had 'lost the hammer blow of simplicity', Lawson was recognising the nature of his art, the power of art in itself and its capacity to deliver truths as pungent and as revealing as those arising from scholarship and research.

Lawson was given a State Funeral because even the bureaucrats vaguely saw that he had said important things, important *Australian* things, in a memorable way that would probably outlast them and their descendants. And, indeed, here we are at the start of the twenty-first century and Henry Lawson, who in his saturnine verses and magnificent stories wrote 'for' Australia with all his heart, remains somehow central to much that we mean and aspire to when we use the word 'Australian'. We argue the toss endlessly about this, but it seems fair to say that, by virtue of the profundity and power of his fiction, Lawson identified and then 'fixed' for us some at least of the ideas we have about our national 'character' and its connections with where and how we live.

This brief anatomy of Lawson makes clear that, in implicitly claiming her degree from the 'University of Hard Knocks', Pauline Hanson should have her credentials investigated. Adherents and graduates of UHK may be impatient of theory, may over-emphasise the practical, may resort to 'experience' as if it is infallible, but they are not ignorant and they do not aggressively champion ignorance. So many of our Great Depression-bred forebears were graduates of UHK through lack of choice, but ignorance was the last thing they wanted or tolerated. One of the several frightening things about the first important manifestation of the One Nation phenomenon was the ignorance of its official views and yet the alacrity with which these views were espoused by what appeared to be a fair proportion of the population. One Nation's positions on race, trade, the economy, education, arts policy, foreign aid and foreign policy were simply a codification of prejudices, hearsay and received 'wisdom' that had been on hand and intermittently adopted, paraded, dropped again, in and out of fashion, for decades. The really critical misinformation and profound ignorance that distinguished One Nation at its executive and rank and file levels (a phenomenon never seriously approached by the media except in the form of jibes and derision), seemed to me to be a sign that we were reaping the 'reward' for decades of educational cut-backs, rejections, serial governmental savaging of both the secondary and tertiary education sectors, and the frequent official encouragement of anti-intellectual and anti-specialist knowledge stances. Note, for example, the Prime Minister's invariable dismissal of objection with the opinion that people are 'sick and tired' of the wharf dispute/Wik/native title/gloomy and uncomfortable history, *et al.*; the implication being they want to get on with a life of mindless relaxation and comfort. (It is not only the present Prime Minister who has spoken and acted in this way, of course: over the past twenty years or so most politicians, state and federal, with only a few honourable exceptions, have enthusiastically attacked academe and academics and have done almost nothing to help state primary and secondary teachers assume a professional role in society.)

When I put this view about a possible connection between One Nation and the dismantling of the education system at a forum held during One Nation's first ascendancy, it was suggested to me that One Nation followers were proud of their lack of education, their aggressive disjunction from the educated. This was probably true, but if it was, it only *reinforced* the point that the education system must have catastrophically failed a whole wedge of the population since the Second World War for such attitudes to be celebrated. When a nation begins seriously to fail in the education of its population, it not only risks subverting the genius of the people, but also eventually produces *a different kind of people*. An increasingly ill-informed, narrowly referenced populace – a subtly different and much less likeable Australia – may well be the emerging harvest from decades of savage education cuts and constraints at secondary school level, just as surely as the current degradation of the idea of the university has been the product of years of official anti-intellectualism, slashed resources and the rampant managerialism that moves into the vacuum left by withdrawn funds and demoralised academics. We hear much of a continuing budget surplus and of the strategies that are crucial to its protection. But this is not the first treasury trove in the last fifty years to be substantially swelled by persistent attacks on tertiary and secondary education funding, among other targets.

One Nation fed off the well-attested and often officially encouraged Australian tendency to anti-intellectualism. But One Nation's anti-intellectualism was not, after all, the latest version of those old and vaguely honourable even if pointless arguments between theory and practice, experience and book-learning, hard yakka and ivory towers. On the contrary: One Nation hated intellect and learning and despised the learned; it had no time for art and culture (products of intellect and imagination) and would have totally abolished financial support for them; it was wary of sophistication and, because it existed through grievance, resentment and aggressively nurtured mental narrowness, it did not entertain the idea of compassion, so racism and the abolition of foreign aid among other inhumanities followed logically. A world view so stripped of spiritual resources was inevitably inward looking, beset by imagined conspiracy, self-consuming; its strongest positives were weapons for self protection (the gun lobby), death as retribution and revenge (capital punishment), and profound suspicion of the world beyond (xenophobia and fortress Australia).

Henry Lawson was not, as Manning Clark once claimed, 'Australia writ large'; but Lawson's 'Australia' – imagined and sketched over a powerful and surviving body of work – constitutes one of the many sites from which important aspects of our cultural heritage may arguably emanate (even if such an idea is subject to constant dispute); which is why his example is a useful counterpoint. As the comparison with even a rather misanthropic Henry Lawson shows, the One Nation position was a long way from any of the traits, besetting flaws, moral stances, cultural provenance or myths and legends that we debate when we grapple with the phenomenon of being white

Australians. Indeed, One Nation stood against them because it had no interest in – was actively antipathetic to – culture broadly or narrowly defined. As its elected Queensland parliamentary incumbents showed before they disintegrated into disaffection and acrimony, One Nation was not a version of some rediscovered tough Australian pragmatism: it was anarchic. Neither its leaders nor its rank and file knew where it would go next or on the back of which half-understood, vaguely apprehended proposition. It was not ideological anarchism but chaotic grievance. It was anarchy as Alexander Pope meant it when he imagined the 'Great Anarch' letting 'the curtain fall/And universal Dullness [covering] all'.

This reference to an eighteenth-century English poem about the threat which ignorance posed to the good order of things is not as mad as it may seem: One Nation is *un*-Australian in so profound a way that Pauline Hanson herself doesn't understand it; we should hope that we do not see its like again.

270

contributors'
biographies

CARMEL BIRD is a fiction writer who grew up in Tasmania. Her writing reflects her passionate interest in the history and culture of her place of origin. Her books include: *Red Shoes*; *Crisis*; *The Bluebird Cafe*; *The White Garden* and *Dear Writer*. She edited *The Penguin Century of Australian Stories* and *The Stolen Children – Their Stories*.

Her website *www.carmelbird.com* is updated every month.

GARY CREW is one of Australia's most awarded writers for youth. He has won the Children's Book Council Children's Book of the Year Award four times, the National Children's Book Award, the NSW Premier's Award, the Victorian Premier's Award and twice been shortlisted for the Edgar Allan Poe Mystery Fiction Award in the United States. Gary lectures in Creative Writing at the University of the Sunshine Coast, Queensland.

GREG DENING prefers to characterise himself as writer of true stories rather than as a professor of history and anthropology, but at present he is Adjunct Professor at the Centre for Cross-Cultural Research, ANU. He 'adjuncts' by conducting postgraduate courses in 'The Creative Imagination in the Presentation of Knowledge'. They are called: 'Challenges to Perform: Seeing, Hearing, Writing, Reflecting'. His own creative imagination is to be found in such books as *Mr Bligh's Bad Language*, *The Death of William Gooch*, *Performances*, and his latest, *Readings/Writings*.

DELIA FALCONER is a Melbourne novelist, essayist, and critic. Her novel *The Service of Clouds* (Picador, 1997) was shortlisted for major Australian awards including the Miles Franklin. Recent publications include *The Penguin Century of Short Stories*, *Best Australian Essays* 1998 and 1999 and *Best Australian Stories* 1999.

BEVERLEY FARMER's books are *Alone, Milk, Home Time, Place of Birth, A Body of Water, The Seal Woman, The House in the Light* and *Collected Stories*. She has one son. During her marriage she spent some years in her husband's village in Greece. She now lives on the Victorian coast.

LUCY FROST is a writer, reviewer and critic whose works include *No Place for a Nervous Lady*, *A Face in the Glass*, *The Journal of Annie Baxter Dawbin*, *Wilde Eve: Eve Langley's Story* and (with Marion Halligan) *The Women Who Go to Hotels*. She is Professor of English at the University of Tasmania.

BILL GAMMAGE grew up in Wagga Wagga, NSW, worked on district wheat harvests for many years, and still likes to go bush. With Bruce Simpson he interviewed more than 30 drovers at Camooweal, Queensland, and recently he crossed the Murranji. He works at the ANU. His books include *The Broken Years: Australian Soldiers in the Great War, Narrandera Shire,* and *The Sky Travellers: Journeys in New Guinea 1938-9.*

LIBBY GLEESON has been shortlisted eight times for the Children's Book Council of Australia Awards across all fiction categories. *Hannah Plus One* was the CBCA Book of the Year, Younger Readers in 1997. *The Great Bear,* illustrated by Armin Greder won the Bologna Ragazzi Award in 2000. This was the first time an Australian book has won this prestigious international award. Libby has been Chair of the Australian Society of Authors, 1999-2001.

PETER GOLDSWORTHY was born in Minlaton, South Australia. His novels have sold more than a quarter of a million copies in Australia alone, and have been translated into most major Asian and European languages. His first collection of poetry, *Readings from Ecclesiastes,* won the Commonwealth Poetry Prize, the Ann Elder award, and the S.A. Premier's Prize. His second, *This Goes With This,* won the Australian Bicentennial Poetry Prize in 1988, jointly with Philip Hodgins.

TOM GRIFFITHS is the author of *Hunters and Collectors: The Antiquarian Imagination in Australia* (Cambridge University Press, 1996), which won the Victorian and New South Wales Premiers' Prizes for Non Fiction in 1996 and the Eureka Science Book Prize. He is a Senior Fellow in the History

Program of the Research School of Social Sciences at the Australian National University, and his latest book is *Forests of Ash: An environmental history* (Cambridge, 2001).

RODNEY HALL has won the Miles Franklin Award twice. His books are published in Australia, USA, UK, Canada, and as translations in six European languages, as well as Chinese and Korean. His most recent novel, *The Day we had Hitler Home* (2000), is the final volume of a septet which presents a metaphorical history of Australia.

MARION HALLIGAN was born in Newcastle on the east coast of Australia and grew up by the sea. Her novels include *Spider Cup*, *Lovers' Knots*, *Wishbone* and *The Golden Dress*. *Eat My Words* and *Cockles of the Heart* are books of autobiography, travel and food. She has published stories in magazines, journals and anthologies, as well as in books like *The Worry Box*, and her *Collected Stories* was published in March 1997. She has written a children's book called *The Midwife's Daughters*. Her most recent novel is *The Fog Garden*, Allen and Unwin, March 2001.

ELIZABETH JOLLEY was born in the industrial midlands of England. She moved to Western Australia in 1959. She has received an Order of Australia, honorary doctorates from WAIT (now Curtin University) and Macquarie and Queensland universities, and the ASAL Gold medal for her contribution to Australian literature. Jolley's work includes short fiction, radio drama, a collection of essays, and 15 novels and collections of short stories. Her novel, *The Well* won the Miles Franklin Award. *Mr Scobie's Riddle* and *My Father's Moon*, won the Age Book of the Year Award, and *The George's Wife*, the National Book award for Fiction.

BRIAN MATTHEWS, who is Visiting Professor and Director of the Europe-Australia Institute at Victoria University, Melbourne, is well known as a scholar in the field of Australian literature, as a columnist for *The Australian Magazine*, and as a writer of fiction, biography and autobiography. He has won various awards, including the Victorian and NSW Premiers' literary prizes, the Gold Medal of the Australian Literature Society and the John Hetherington Bicentennial Biography Prize (shared). His most recent books are *A Fine and Private Place*, Picador 2000 and *As The Story Goes*, Text 2001.

LES MURRAY is Australia's leading poet. He has published some thirty books. His work is studied in schools and universities around Australia and has been translated into more than ten foreign languages. He has received numerous awards, including the T.S. Eliot Prize for poetry for his collection *Subhuman Redneck Poems*, and the Queen's Medal for Poetry for *Fredy Neptune*.

DOROTHY PORTER has published ten books, including five collections of poetry and three verse novels. Her most recent verse novel, *What a Piece of Work*, was the first book of poetry to be short-listed for the Miles Franklin Award. Her crime thriller *The Monkey's Mask* has recently been made into a feature film.

CASSANDRA PYBUS is the author of seven books including *Community of Thieves* about the last tribal people of Tasmania, *Gross Moral Turpitude*, which won the 1994 Colin Roderick Award, *White Rajah: A Dynastic Intrigue* and her memoir *Till Apples Grow on an Orange Tree*. Her highly controversial biography, *The Devil and James McAuley*, won the Adelaide Festival Award for Non Fiction in 2000. *Raven Road*, which is set in the sub-arctic regions of North America, will be published in 2001. Cassandra is the founding editor of *Australian Humanities Review* and holds an Australian Research Council Senior Fellowship at the University of Tasmania.

HENRY REYNOLDS is an historian who is currently Research Professor at the University of Tasmania. The winner of the 1999 Australian Human Rights Award for the Arts. Henry is the author of ten books including *Why Weren't We Told?*, *The Whispering in our Hearts* and *The Other Side of the Frontier*. *Black Pioneers* (an updated version of *With the White People*) was released in October 2000.

ALEXIS WRIGHT is a member of the Waanyi people of the southern highlands of the Gulf of Carpentaria. She is the author of *Grog War*, and the novel *Plains of Promise* (UQP), 1997.

notes

Gary Crew

Godard, P. *The First and Last Voyage of the* Batavia. Abrolhos Publishing. 1993.

Eldridge, C.C. *Context and Commentary: The Imperial Experience.* Macmillan Press. 1996.

Crew, G. *Strange Objects.* Hodder. 2001.

Hanson, Neil. *The Custom of the Sea.* Random House. 1999.

Sayce, C. *The Splendid Savage.* Thomas Nelson, n.d. Inscribed 1926.

Idriess, I. *Headhunters of the Coral Sea* . Angus and Robertson. 1944.

Dixon, R. *Writing the Colonial Adventure.* Cambridge University Press. 1995.

Drake-Brockman, H. *Voyage to Disaster.* Angus and Robertson. 1963.

Edwards, H. *The Wreck of the Half Moon Reef.* Angus and Robertson.

Edge, A. *The Company.* Picador. 2000.

Bowen Historical Society. *The Story of James Morrill.* n.d. Bowen, Qld.

Holthouse, H. *Ships In the Coral.* Macmillan. 1976.

Ingleton, G. *True Patriots All.* Charles E. Tuttle. 1988.

McIntyre, K. *The Secret Discovery of Australia.* Souvenir Press, 1977.

King, Stephen. *Danse Macabre.* Macdonald and Co. 1981.

Saxby, M. *Offered to Children.* Scholastic, Australia. 1998.

Favenc, E. *Marooned on Australia.* Blackie and Son. 1896.

Collingridge, G. *The Discovery of Australia.* Golden Press. 1983.

Millar, A. *I See No End to Travelling.* Bay Books. n.d. Sydney.

Gideon, S. *The Eternal Present.* OUP. 1962.

Gerritsen, R. *And Their Ghosts May be Heard.* Fremantle Arts Centre Press. 1994.

Beverley Farmer

Prichard, Katharine Susannah. *Coonardoo (The Well in the Shadow).* Angus & Robertson, Sydney, 1964.

Throssell, Ric. *Wild Weeds and Windflowers: the Life and Letters of Katharine Susannah Prichard.* Angus & Robertson, Sydney, 1975.

Lucy Frost

American Poetry 'A Trucanini Photo Gallery'
http://www.english.uiuc.edu/maps/poets/m_r/rose/trucaniniphotos.htm

Anderson, Ian, 'Re-claiming Tru-ger-nan-ner: De-colonising the symbol', *Art Monthly Australia*, 66 (1993–4), pp. 10–14.

Dixon, Christine, 'Benjamin Duterrau', in Joan Kerr, ed., *The Dictionary of Australian Artists.* Melbourne: Oxford University Press, 1992, pp. 231–3.

Dubin, Steven C. *Displays of Power: Memory and Amnesia in the American Museum.* New York: New York University Press, 1999.

Graves, J. W. 'Trucanini's Story of Herself: Letter to the Editor', *The Mercury,* 6 June 1876, p. 3.

McGregor, Russell, *Imagined Destinies: Aboriginal Australians and the doomed race theory, 1880-1939.* Carlton, Vic: Melbourne University Press, 1997.

Petrow, Stefan, 'The Last Man: The Mutilation of William Lanne in 1869 and its aftermath', *Aboriginal History* 21 (1997), pp. 90–112.

O'Regan, Tom, 'Documentary in Controversy: *The Last Tasmanian*' 1984; rpt. Albert Moran and Tom O'Regan, eds., *An Australian Film Reader.* Sydney: Currency Press, 1985, pp 127–136.

Pybus, Cassandra, *Community of Thieves.* Melbourne: William Heinemann Australia, 1991.

Rae Ellis, Vivienne, *Trucanini: Queen or Traitor?* Canberra: Australian Institute of Aboriginal Studies, 1981.

Reynolds, Henry, *Fate of a Free People.* Ringwood, Vic: Penguin, 1995.

Bill Gammage

Peter Dermoudy, 'A Survey of Historic Sites: Elsey Cemetery', unpublished 1988 (courtesy Mataranka Community Council.

'Mrs Aeneas Gunn' (*Australian Dictionary of Biography* file, Canberra).

Mrs Aeneas Gunn, *The Little Black Princess,* Melbourne 1905, and *We of the Never-Never,* London 1908.

Francesca Merlan (comp), *Big River Country. Stories from Elsey Station,* Alice Springs 1996

Ira Nesdale, *The Little Missus,* Adelaide 1977.

Bruce Simpson, *The Packhorse Drover,* ABC Books, 1996.

Wild Life, June 1944.

Tom Griffiths

Brown Harrison, Woodward EL, Toynbee Arnold J and Ratcliffe SK *Our Neighbours: Today and Yesterday,* Germany, France, Russia, The United States, Gerald Hore Ltd, London, 1933.

Griffiths, Tom and Robin, Libby (eds) *Ecology and Empire: Environmental History of Settler Societies,* Keele University Press, Edinburgh, 1997.

Oakman, Daniel 'The Seed of Freedom: Regional Security and the Colombo Plan', *Australian Journal of Politics and History,* vol. 46, no. 1, March 2000.

Ratcliffe, Francis *Flying Fox and Drifting Sand,* Angus & Robertson, Sydney, 1947.

Ratcliffe, Francis 'The Flying Fox (Pteropus) in Australia', *Bulletin,* no. 15, Melbourne: CSIRO, 1931.

Alexis Wright

See pages 23-24, referring to correspondence Hann had with anthropologists Howitt (19.8.1881), that the Inspector of Native Police, Lamond told him that police had shot 100 blacks in 3 years alone around this (Lawn Hills) run. Appendix A: A brief history of Aboriginal associations with the Lawn Hills area, prepared for Doomadgee Aboriginal Council, by Dr D. Trigger & Dr J. Devitt, Consulting Anthropologists, 20 January, 1993.

Whitefella Comin', David S. Trigger, CUP, 1992, p.26.

This information is contained in the Nicholson River (Waanyi/Garawa) Land Claim Book, Northern Land Council, 1982.

See Map 3, p. 28, *Whitefella Comin'*, David S. Trigger, CUP, 1992.

Whitefella Comin', David S. Trigger, CUP, 1992, p.31.

See Appendix A: A brief history of Aboriginal associations with the Lawn Hills area, prepared by Dr D. Trigger & Dr J. Devitt, for the Doomadgee Aboriginal Council, January 1992.

See page 27, Appendix A: A brief history of Aboriginal association with the Lawn Hills area, prepared by Dr D. Trigger & Dr J. Devitt, for the Doomadgee Aboriginal Council, January 1992.

Telephone conversation with Carmal Wagstaff of Brunette Downs on the August 1999.

The 1898 marriage certificate of Opal and Sam Ah Bow.

How Many Grids To Gregory? compiled by the Gregory Branch QCWA in 1977, p. 13.

Records of E.M. Thornton, Office of Protector of Aboriginals, Gregory Downs, 1930s.

(Exhibit 45). page 23, Report by Mr Justice Kearney for the Nicholson River (Waanyi/Garawa) Land Claim. Justice Kearney accepted this evidence of descent and applied to the group being 'local' under the Act, even though it was obvious under the historical circumstances only few of the claimants resided on the country they claimed.

Dr John Morton, in *Heritage of Namatjira, The Watercolours of Central Australia*, ed. J. Hardy, J.V.S. Megaw & R. Megaw, William Heinemann Australia, Melbourne, 1992, pp. 32–34.

acknowledgements

Thanks to the Word Festival committee, and in particular Judy Pearce, for the work they put into the conception and execution of this project. Gratitude also for the participation of the National Museum of Australia, and especially Colin MacDougall, whose help in collecting and collating the images has been invaluable.

Pearl shell Phallocrypt (cover), artist unknown, 1975, Western Australia, NMA collection. Photograph: George Serras, ©NMA. *Ship Wheel* (p 14), on loan from the South Australian Maritime Museum. Photograph: George Serras, ©NMA. *Handheld Sextant* (p 30), c.1840, on loan from Consulting Surveyors Australia. Photograph: George Serras, ©NMA. *Chromo plate XIII* (p46) from William Saville-Kent, *Great Barrier Reef Mollusca and Planarians*, W.H. Allen, London 1893, NMA collection. Photograph: George Serras, ©NMA. *Refined Mutton Bird Oil* (p56), Tasmania, NMA collection. Photograph: Gerald Preiss, ©NMA. *Jewel of the Sea* (p68), mariner shell necklace, Corrie Fullard, 1997, Flinders Island, Tasmania, NMA collection. Photograph: Steve Keough, ©Australian Heritage Museum. *Bark Basket* (p94), artist unknown, date unknown, Western Australia, NMA collection. Photograph: George Serras, ©NMA. *The Crimson-Sided Snake (Coluber Porphyriacus)* (p104) from George Shaw's *Zoology and Botany of New Holland and the Isles Adjacent*, London 1794, Page 26, ©NMA. Photograph: George Serras, ©NMA. *Monaro Corrugations* (p108), corrugated iron shearing shed, Monaro, NSW. Photograph: ©2000 Maureen Mackenzie-Taylor. *Breast Collar* (p124), saddlery, NMA collection. Photograph: George Serras, ©NMA. *Parched earth* (p132), Willandra Lakes, NSW. Photograph: ©1996 Benita Tunks. *Flying Foxes (detail)*, (p144), ochres on bark, Mick Gubargu, date unknown, Maningrida, Northern Territory, NMA collection. Photograph: Matt Kelso, ©NMA. *Lattice* (p176), marine apartments, Grange, South Australia, NMA collection. Photograph: George Serras, ©NMA. *Franca stationmaster's fob watch* (p178), Switzerland, c.1920. Photograph: George Serras, ©NMA. *Emmco electric food mixer* (p192), 1935, NMA collection. Photograph: George Serras, ©NMA. *Abelard to Eloisa* (p206), Walter Lehmann, in *The Bulletin*, August 5 1961, courtesy of the National Library of Australia. *Flaked stone knife blade* (p222), proximal half covered in adhesive, creator unknown, date unknown, Waanyi region, Nicholson River, Northern Territory, NMA collection. Photograph: George Serras, ©NMA. *Author's Grandmother* (p240), Photograph: ©Phyllis Ah Kit. *Selection of Westerly magazines* (p242), 1983-1985, courtesy of Marion Halligan. Photograph: George Serras, ©NMA. *"The Thin Black Line," or Our Northern Coast Defence* (p256). Cartoon by Alf Vincent, in *The Bulletin* 18 July 1907, courtesy of the National Library of Australia.